Welsh Calendar Cookbook

by

G i l l i   D a v i e s

First impression: 2005
Second impression: 2011

© Y Lolfa Cyf. and Gilli Davies

Book and cover design: Olwen Fowler

ISBN: 086243 749 0

Printed and published in Wales by
Y Lolfa Cyf., Talybont, Ceredigion, SY24 5HE
e-mail ylolfa@ylolfa.com
website www.ylolfa.com
tel. (01970 832304)
fax (01970 832782)

Welsh Calendar Cookbook

by

Gilli Davies

yLolfa

Spring

If the Ash comes out before the oak
Then we'll surely have a soak.
If the Oak comes out before the ash
Then we'll only have a splash

The arrival of spring always brings welcome new flavours to the kitchen: bright green spring vegetables, pretty pink rhubarb and the best of the shellfish to enjoy, and there are recipes to brighten up the appetite. With the daffodils out, a feast of lamb and leeks to prepare for St David's day, and Easter just around the corner, there is surely much to celebrate at this time of year.

Mussel Broth
(Cawl cregyn gleision)

900g (2lbs) fresh mussels in their shells
1 medium onion, chopped
2 cloves garlic, crushed with salt
12g (½ oz) butter
75g (3oz) fresh white breadcrumbs
1 tablespoon lemon juice
100 ml (4fl oz) dry white wine
4 tablespoons cream, single or double
2 tablespoon parsley, chopped

1. Scrub the mussels thoroughly, place in a large pan and cover completely with cold water. Bring to the boil and cook until the shells open – approximately 3 minutes.
2. Strain the liquid from the mussels and boil it hard, to reduce it to 900ml (1½ pints).
3. Meanwhile, remove the top shells and the little weed or 'beard' from the mussels, discarding any mussels that are stubborn to open.
4. In a separate saucepan cook the onion and garlic gently in the butter. Pour on the reduced mussel juice and add the breadcrumbs, lemon juice and wine. Bring to the boil and return the mussels to the soup to reheat.
5. Add the cream and the parsley, but don't let the soup boil, or the cream will curdle.
6. Ladle the mussels into soup bowls, pour the broth over and serve immediately.
7. This makes a good meal in itself, and I suggest that you put a basket of hot crusty bread and some butter on the table to complete the meal.

Leek and Potato Soup
(Cawl cennin a thatws)

I rasher bacon, diced
25g (Ioz) butter
2 large leeks, washed and chopped
450g (Ilb) potatoes, peeled and diced
900ml (1½ pints) chicken stock
300 ml (½ pint) milk
2 tablespoons parsley, chopped
salt and freshly ground black pepper
lemon juice to taste (optional)

To garnish
cream
chopped parsley

1. In a large saucepan fry the diced bacon in the butter. Add the leeks and potatoes and cook gently for 5 minutes.
2. Pour in the stock and milk, bring to the boil, and continue to simmer for 20 minutes.
3. Cool slightly, then liquidize and season to taste, adding a squeeze of lemon juice if the flavour is too bland.
4. To serve, pour the soup into bowls, swirl a spoonful of cream into each one and add a sprinkling of parsley.
5. As a main meal soup, serve unblended, leaving the pieces of bacon and vegetable intact, with, perhaps, a bowl of grated Cheddar cheese or even some slices of frankfurter sausage added.
6. NB: For an iced summer soup, try adding a dash of cold white wine.

Deep-fried
Laver Seaweed

100g (4oz) laver seaweed	paprika pepper
flour	ground coriander seed
vegetable oil for deep-frying	salt

1. Wash the laver seaweed thoroughly to remove any sand. Leave the seaweed to drain in a colander and then dry thoroughly.
2. Tear the laver into strips, dip in flour and shake off the excess.
3. Deep-fry the laver in moderately hot oil for about 2–3 minutes until crisp.
4. Sprinkle with paprika and freshly ground coriander and salt. Serve as a nibble with drinks.

Baked Oysters
with Bacon

12 oysters, freshly removed from the shell
12 rashers of dry cured, smoked, streaky, Welsh bacon

1. Stretch out the bacon using the back of a knife.
2. Roll the oysters in the streaky bacon and secure with a cocktail stick.
3. Grill the oysters wrapped in bacon under a hot grill so that the bacon is crisp and the oysters inside are lightly cooked through.
4. Serve as part of an hors d'oeuvres or as a cocktail nibble.

Leek, Egg and Welsh Cheese Tartlets

To make 24 tartlets

350g (12oz) plain flour
pinch of salt
175g (6oz) mixed butter and white vegetable fat
a little cold water to mix

The filling

100g (4oz) bacon, ideally smoked streaky, diced
1 small leek, washed and chopped
300ml (½ pint) mixed milk and cream
2 whole eggs
2 egg yolks
100g (4oz) mature Welsh cheddar, grated
salt and freshly ground black pepper

First make the pastry:

1. Tip the flour into a large bowl and add the salt. Cut the fat into cubes and drop them into the flour. Rub the fat into the flour, using your fingertips and lifting the mixture up and away from the bowl. (This will help to keep the pastry cool). Alternatively, use a food processor.

2. When you have a mixture that looks like breadcrumbs, pour in enough water to amalgamate the pastry to form a dough. Knead for 1 minute, until it is smooth and even in texture and colour, then, chill in the fridge for ½ hour.

Make the filling:

3. Beat all the eggs together. Dry-fry the diced bacon until the fat runs and the bacon begins to brown and crisp. Add the leek and cook until soft, then remove the pan from the heat and add the creamy milk, eggs and grated cheese. Stir well and add seasoning to taste.

4. Roll out the pastry and, using a pastry cutter, line 24 small tartlet cases.

5. Ladle the mixture into the pastry cases, making sure that there is an even mixture of bacon and leek to the egg and cheese custard.

6. Bake in a hot oven, 220°c, Gas 7, for 10–12 minutes or until brown and crisp.

7. Serve warm.

Leek, Egg and Welsh Cheese Tartlets

Queen Scallops pan fried with Laver bread

Queen Scallops pan fried with Laver bread, Welsh Wine and Cream

450g (1lb) queen scallops
25g (1oz) butter
1 tablespoon laver bread
$\frac{1}{2}$ orange, grated rind
1 glass dry white wine,
    Welsh if possible
1 tablespoon double cream
    or crème fraiche

1. Clean the scallops and dry on kitchen paper, leaving the little orange corals attached wherever possible.
2. In a large frying pan heat the butter until it sizzles. Fry the scallops, a few at a time, adding more butter if necessary. Fry briskly to cook on all sides, then remove from the pan and arrange in individual serving dishes.
3. Add the laver bread to the pan with the orange rind and wine. Boil up well, taste for seasoning and add the cream.
4. Pour the sauce over the scallops and serve immediately.
5. Serve with fresh herb rolls.

Fish and Shellfish
Skate with Wild Garlic Butter

675g (1½ lb) skate
juice of ½ lemon
1 tablespoon oil
25g (1 oz) butter

Garlic Butter
75g (3oz) unsalted butter
juice of ½ lemon
1 level tablespoon chopped wild garlic
    leaves or 1 clove garlic, crushed
    to a paste with a little salt

1. Cut the skate into manageable pieces.
2. Heat the oil and butter in a large frying pan and as soon as it foams put in the skate pieces. Fry over a medium heat for 3–5 minutes, turn and cook the other side.
3. Carefully lift the cooked skate out of the pan and transfer to a warm serving dish.
4. To make the garlic butter, put the unsalted butter in the frying-pan and heat it over a fast flame until it foams and begins to turn brown. Add the squeezed lemon juice at once, toss in the chopped garlic leaves and pour over the skate.
5. Serve immediately, with fresh boiled noodles to soak up the butter sauce.

11

Teifi Fish Bake

Teifi Fish Bake

675g (1½ lb) potatoes,
   cooked and diced
350g (12oz) each cod fillet
   and smoked haddock fillet,
   skinned and cubed

600ml (1pint) mornay sauce,
   made with 25g butter,
   25g flour and 1 pint of milk
60ml (4 tablespoons) parsley,
   freshly chopped
25g (1oz) Teifi cheese, grated

1. Place the fish in an ovenproof dish.
2. Mix the sauce with the chopped parsley and pour over the fish.
3. Top with diced potato and the reserved cheese.
4. Bake for 25 minutes at 200°c, Gas mark 6.
5. Garnish with parsley.

Whole Poached Sewin with Sorrel and Laver bread Mayonnaise

1.8–2.7kg (4–6lb) sewin or salmon, whole fish with head and tail
watercress, lemon wedges and cucumber to garnish

Sorrel and Laver bread Seaweed Mayonnaise
300ml (½ pint) home-made mayonnaise, or 1 jar best mayonnaise
1 good handful fresh sorrel, chopped
1 teaspoon laver bread, tinned or fresh (a tablespoonful
  of pesto sauce makes a good alternative)
1 good tablespoon fresh dill, chopped
1 good tablespoon chives, chopped

1. Poach the salmon in gently simmering salt water for 4–6 minutes per pound. Remove the pan from the stove and leave for ½ hour before removing salmon from the water.

Alternatively, you can parcel the salmon in buttered tinfoil with half a glass of white wine, salt, peppercorns and several slices of lemon, and bake in a moderate oven 180°c, Gas mark 4, for ½ hour.

2. Do not unwrap for 10 minutes or so after removing from the oven. Skin the fish, remove the head and tail and keep to one side. Then, carefully lift all four fillets off the bone, and wrap each individually in foil until required.

3. Mix all the herbs and laver bread into the mayonnaise; taste for seasoning.

To serve
On a large oval serving dish, reassemble the two underside fillets of salmon and spread a layer of mayonnaise over the top. Place the upper fillets on top and reposition the head and tail. Garnish with thinly sliced cucumber round the head and down the length of the fish. Add lemon slices and bunches of watercress. Serve the remaining mayonnaise separately.

13

Honey-roast leg of Welsh Lamb

Meat, Poultry and Offal

Honey-roast leg of Welsh Lamb with Cider, Ginger and Rosemary

1 leg of Welsh lamb weighing
about 1.5kg (3lb 5oz)
2.5cm (1inch) piece of fresh
root ginger
25g (1oz) butter, melted
2 tablespoons honey
1 tablespoon fresh rosemary,
finely chopped
250ml (9 fl oz) dry cider
salt and freshly ground
black pepper

1. Peel the ginger and cut into slivers. Using a sharp knife, make small cuts in the leg of lamb and insert the ginger.
2. Mix the butter, honey and rosemary together and spread over the lamb.
3. Place in a roasting tin, pour in half of the cider, and cover loosely with foil. Roast in a moderately hot oven, 190°c, Gas mark 5, allowing 25 minutes per pound.
4. When three-quarters cooked, remove the foil and continue cooking, basting frequently with the juices in the roasting tin and adding more cider if necessary.
5. Remove the joint from the oven, lift out of the pan and keep warm. Strain the juices from the pan, removing any excess fat and pour in the rest of the cider to 'deglaze' the pan. Boil this up well, return the non-fatty juices and thicken with a little corn flour or arrowroot, if you wish.
6. A well-seasoned, mixed mash of carrot, parsnip, turnip and potatoes tastes perfect with the roast lamb.

Welsh Beef, Beer and Rosemary Cobbler

1kg (2.2lbs) beef (stewing or shin)
seasoned plain flour
50g (2oz) dripping or
    2 tablespoons cooking oil
2 onions, peeled and diced
2 leeks, washed and sliced
2 carrots, scrubbed and sliced
300ml (½ pint) beef stock
300ml (½ pint) brown ale
2 teaspoons fresh rosemary, finely chopped
1 tablespoon tomato puree

For the scone topping
75g (3oz) butter
225g (8oz) self-raising flour
salt
1 teaspoon rosemary, finely chopped
1 egg
milk to mix

1. Pre-heat the oven to 150°c, Gas mark 2.
2. Cut the fat and sinew off the beef and dice into 2.5cm (1 inch) chunks. Toss in the seasoned flour. Heat the dripping or oil in a heavy-based casserole and fry the meat, a little at a time so that it browns on all sides.
3. Remove from the pan and fry the onions, leeks and carrots gently until they colour.
4. Replace the beef and add the liquid, herbs and tomato puree. Cover and cook gently for 2 hours.

The scone topping

1. Rub the butter into the flour, stir in the salt and herbs.
2. Mix the beaten egg with a little milk and add to the flour to make a soft dough.
3. Roll or pat out the dough on a floured surface. Cut into circles with a small cutter.
4. Remove the casserole from the oven and increase the heat to 220°c, Gas mark 7. Place the scones, overlapping one another, on top of the meat.
5. Brush with milk, return to the hot oven and bake for 10–15 minutes until the crust is golden brown.

Welsh Breakfast with Bacon, Laver Cakes, and Cockles with Eggs

It may seem a little unusual to eat seaweed for breakfast, but miners enjoyed this traditional Welsh breakfast before a day down the pit. The flavours are rich and strong and certainly set you up for the day!

Fry some dry cured bacon gently, so that the fat runs and flavours the pan. Take the bacon from the pan and keep warm while you fry the laver cakes in the bacon fat. Add these to the bacon and keep warm, finally cooking the cockles and eggs in the remnants of the bacon juices. Serve at once.

Laver Cakes
100g (4oz) fresh or
  tinned laver bread
25g (1oz) medium or
  fine oatmeal

Mix the laver bread and the oatmeal together and shape into little rissole-like cakes about 5cm (2") across and 2cm (½") thick. Slide the laver cakes into the hot bacon fat and fry fairly quickly for 2–3 minutes on each side, shaping and patting the cakes with a palette knife as they fry. Lift out carefully.

Cockles with Eggs
175g (6oz) fresh cooked
  cockles, out of shell
2 eggs, beaten
freshly milled black
  pepper

Fry the cockles in a little bacon fat for a few minutes then pour over the beaten eggs. Stir well with a wooden spoon until the egg is lightly cooked. Season with pepper.

Alternative ways to serve eggs
Boiled, fried or poached and served with laver cakes. Scrambled with a little laver bread in the mixture. Fried with a couple of cockles dropped into the white for colour.

Baked Chicken wrapped in Bacon with Leek and Tarragon Sauce

4 skinless breasts of chicken
8 rashers smoked back bacon
2 large leeks, thinly sliced
600ml (1 pint) milk
150ml (½ pint) chicken stock
50g (2oz) butter
50g (2oz) plain flour
2 tablespoons chopped fresh tarragon
   or ½ tablespoon dried tarragon
salt and pepper

1. Wrap each breast of chicken in 2 rashers of bacon, overlapping so that the ends are underneath.

2. Place on a roasting tray and bake for 20–30 minutes, 200°c, Gas mark 5, until the bacon is crisp and the chicken cooked through.

3. Meanwhile, make the sauce. Melt the butter in a thick-bottomed pan and gently fry the leeks until soft. Add the flour and cook for 1 minute, stirring well.

4. Gradually add the milk and stock, stirring constantly until the sauce thickens.

5. Add the tarragon and simmer gently for 4–5 minutes, to cook the flour. Season to taste.

6. Slice the chicken diagonally and arrange on a warmed serving plate, on a pool of leek and tarragon sauce.

Welsh Faggots with Onion Gravy

350g (12 oz) pig's liver
225g (8oz) belly of pork
2 onions, peeled
1 cooking apple, peeled and cored
50g (2oz) fresh breadcrumbs
1 teaspoon chopped sage leaves
a good pinch of nutmeg
a good pinch of ground ginger
salt and freshly milled black pepper
1 egg beaten
pig's or lamb's caul (optional)

1. Soak the caul (if available) in warm water for 20 minutes before using.
2. In a food processor, chop finely the liver, belly of pork, onions and apple. Blend these well with the breadcrumbs, herbs and seasonings, and then bind with the beaten egg.
3. Using wet hands, shape the mixture into round faggots the size of an egg, wrap each in a square of caul and arrange closely together in a baking tray. If you prefer to lay the caul over the top of the faggots, the effect is the same and the process much quicker). If no caul is available, cover the faggots with a layer of well buttered foil and bake in a moderate oven, 180°c, Gas mark 4, for about 45 minutes.
4. Test by piercing the faggots to see if the juices run clear. Towards the end of the cooking time, turn up the heat a little and allow the faggots to brown on top.

Vegetables, Salads and Vegetarian Dishes
Potato Wedges

Onion Gravy

1. Peel and finely chop an onion. Cook it very gently in 25g (1oz) lard, butter or oil until soft and transparent. Turn up the heat and cook the onion until it is a rich brown colour.
2. Stir in a tablespoon of plain flour and continue to cook until the flour has turned a golden brown. Now add 300ml ($^1\!/_2$ pint) of good brown stock and bring to the boil. Season well.

900g (2lb) medium-sized potatoes
1 tablespoon sunflower or safflower oil
sea salt and freshly ground black pepper

For the flavourings
1 clove garlic, crushed
15ml (1 tablespoon) chopped fresh herbs
2.5ml ($^1\!/_2$ teaspoon) cayenne pepper
pinch of curry powder

1. Cut the unpeeled potatoes, first in half, and then into wedges, so that each piece has a good edge of skin and they are all about the same size. Put all the wedges in a plastic bag with the oil and salt and pepper.
2. Add flavourings of your choice, then shake the bag well, so that the potatoes are evenly covered with oil and seasoning.
3. Arrange the wedges in a single layer over 1–2 baking trays. Roast in a pre-heated oven, 220°c, Gas mark 7, for 20 minutes. Turn the wedges over and return to the oven for another 10 minutes.
4. Eat as soon as they come out of the oven.

Ramsons Salad

A good handful of ramsons, (wild garlic leaves) picked at the last minute
1 soft lettuce (lambs, oak-leaf, curly endive, lollo rosso or bianco)
a good handful of mild fresh herbs, such as parsley and marjoram
8 rashers bacon, cooked and snipped small
2 ripe avocado pears, peeled and diced
1 tablespoon pine nuts or sunflower seeds

For the dressing
3 tablespoons best olive oil
1 tablespoon white vinegar or cider vinegar
1 teaspoon honey
1 teaspoon wholegrain mustard
salt and pepper

1. Arrange the lettuce in a large salad bowl.
2. Add the bacon, avocado and nuts. Sprinkle over the fresh herbs and, lastly, snip the ramsons over the top.
3. Mix and shake the ingredients for the dressing, and toss the salad well.

Spinach and Carrot Flan

1 head of spring greens or 12 largish fresh spinach leaves
1 medium onion, peeled and finely chopped
12g (¹/₂oz) butter
1 egg
2 tablespoons double cream
a pinch of ground cumin
salt and freshly ground pepper
225g (8oz) carrots, peeled and finely grated

1. Blanch the spring greens or spinach leaves in a pan of boiling water, then plunge into cold water to retain the bright green colour.

2. Cut off the stems and any strong veins in the leaves, and then use them to line a 6-inch (15 cm) flan dish, overlapping, and leaving enough of the leaves flopping outside the dish to fold back over once the filling is in place.

3. Fry the onion in the butter until soft but not brown.

4. Beat the egg, cream, cumin and seasoning together, then add the cooked onion and grated carrot and mix well. Spoon the mixture into the lined flan dish, cover with the overlapping greens, and wrap the whole dish in foil.

5. Place the wrapped flan dish in a roasting tray with enough water to come halfway up the side of the flan. Bake in a moderate oven preheated to 180°c, Gas mark 4, for 45 minutes. Turn the carrot flan out of the dish and cut into 4 wedges.

Spinach and Carrot Flan

Steamed Leek Puddings

4 good sized leeks
2 slices wholemeal bread
2 eggs

120ml (4fl oz) double cream
salt and pepper
pinch of paprika

pinch of grated fresh ginger
1 tablespoon chopped parsley

1. Split the leeks lengthways and wash well. Plunge them into a shallow pan of boiling water and simmer for a few minutes until soft. Rinse under a cold tap to retain the bright green colour.
2. Using a combination of light and dark green leaves, line four dariole moulds or ramekins. Set aside the remaining leeks.
3. Process or blend the bread to make crumbs. Add the leeks, eggs and double cream and blend until you have a smooth, dropping consistency.
4. Add extra breadcrumbs if the mixture is too runny, or extra milk to soften. Season with paprika, ginger and parsley and place the mixture into the lined moulds.
5. Fold over excess leek leaf to make secure parcels, and steam the moulds, or cook in a bain-marie, for approximately 20 minutes, until firm to touch.

Desserts

Hazelnut Meringue Cake with Black Mountain Liqueur Cream

125g (5ozs) ground roasted hazelnuts
4 egg whites
1 cup castor sugar
1 teaspoon vanilla
1 teaspoon white vinegar
200g dark chocolate, chopped
50g (2ozs) butter

1. Using an electric mixer, whisk the egg whites till stiff.

2. Gradually add the sugar to the beaten egg whites, beating well after each addition.
3. Fold in the vanilla, vinegar and hazelnuts. Pipe into 2 x 23cm circles on 2 oven trays covered with non-stick baking paper.
4. Bake in a moderate oven, 180°c, Gas mark 4, for 25 minutes or until firm.
5. Leave to cool.

Black Mountain Liqueur Cream
125g (5ozs) cream cheese
50g (2ozs) butter
50g (2ozs) caster sugar
2 tablespoons of Black Mountain Liqueur (substitute Cassis)
300ml (10 fl. ozs) whipping cream

1. Beat the cream cheese, butter, and sugar in a small bowl with an electric mixer until light and fluffy.

2. Add the liqueur and cream, and beat until well mixed.

Assembly
1. Melt the chocolate and butter in a bowl over hot water. Spread evenly over the meringue layers. Spread with half the liqueur cream.
2. Top with the other meringue layer, chocolate side down.
3. Spread top and side of cake with remaining liqueur cream.
4. Decorate with shavings of dark chocolate and extra whipped cream if desired.

Honey, Hazelnut and Lemon Mousse
(Mousse o fêl, cnau cyll a lemwn)

3 tablespoons Welsh runny honey
juice of 1 lemon
75g (3oz) hazelnuts,
    finely chopped
2 egg yolks
3 whole eggs
50g (2oz) caster sugar
150ml (5fl oz) double cream
12g (½ oz) gelatine
2 tablespoons mead
    or sweet sherry

To garnish
Whipped cream for piping
Whole hazelnuts

1. Mix the honey, lemon juice and hazelnuts together.
2. Put the egg yolks and whole eggs in a basin with the caster sugar and whisk over gentle heat (sit the basin on top of a saucepan of hot water) until thick and mousse-like.
3. Once thick, cool the mousse as quickly as possible. The best method is to place the bowl in a larger bowl which has been filled with ice cubes or iced water. Then fold in the honey, nuts and lemon juice. Whisk the cream until thick and fold it into the mousse.
4. Dissolve the gelatine in the mead or sherry then pour this into the mousse, stirring gently in a continuous movement to distribute the gelatine evenly. Don't stir too hard or you will knock the lightness out of the mousse.
5. As the mousse begins to set, pour it into a serving bowl or individual dishes. Chill for an hour.
6. Garnish with a swirl of piped whipped cream topped with a whole hazelnut.

Rhubarb Griddle Tarts (*Tarten Planc*) With Strawberry and Elderflower Sauce

For the Pastry
175g (6oz) plain flour
75g (3oz) butter
pinch of salt
water to mix

For the Filling
450g (1lb) rhubarb, sliced
  (gooseberries or cooking
  apples could be used also)
juice of half an orange
honey to sweeten

For the Sauce
225g (8oz) fresh strawberries
1 tablespoon elderflower cordial

The pastry

1. Make up as for short crust, by rubbing the butter into flour and adding just enough cold water to make a firm dough.
2. Leave to rest for ½ hour before rolling out and cutting into discs with a 7.5cm (3") pastry cutter.

For the filling

3. Cook the rhubarb in the orange juice until just tender but still holding shape – ideally, cook it in the microwave. Sweeten with honey. Leave to cool.

For the sauce

Liquidise the strawberries with a tablespoon of elderflower cordial. Sieve the puree and sweeten to taste.

Put 1 tablespoon of the rhubarb on half of the discs and place another disc on top, seal the edges with a little cold water. Press the discs together firmly at the edges. Bake on a griddle over moderate heat, turning carefully to cook both sides. Serve the tarts warm, dredged with caster sugar and surrounded by a spoonful of sauce.

Apple and Pear Fritters

Apple and Pear Fritters

2 whole apples, peeled,
    cored and cut into rings
2 whole pears, peeled,
    cored and cut into rings

Batter
100g (4oz) plain flour
pinch of salt
15 ml (1 tablespoon) oil
150 ml (5 fl ozs) warm water
1 egg white
flour to coat fruit
icing or caster sugar for glaze

1. For the batter, mix the flour, salt and oil with warm water to form a smooth paste.
2. Whisk the egg white until stiff and carefully fold into the batter mixture.
3. Coat the fruit pieces in the flour, then the batter.
4. Deep fry at 180°C for a few minutes, or until lightly browned. Remove and place on absorbent kitchen paper to soak up any excess oil.
5. Dust the tops with sugar, then place under a grill and grill until the sugar has melted, forming an attractive, golden brown glaze.

Baking
Wholemeal Rolls with Gibbons

1.5k (3 lbs) wholemeal flour
1 teaspoon salt
50g (2oz) easy-blend yeast
    or 25g (1oz) fresh yeast
½ teaspoon brown sugar
100g (4oz) gibbons or spring
    onions, chopped green and
    white parts
1 tablespoon parsley, chopped
900ml (1½ pints) warm water
25g (1oz) butter

1. Pre-heat the oven to 220°c, Gas mark 7.
2. Combine the flour and salt in a large mixing bowl and leave in a warm place for about 10 minutes. Sprinkle in the yeast and sugar and stir well. (Fresh yeast must be mixed with a little water first).
3. Pour in the water and mix to a firm dough. Knead by hand or machine for 5 minutes.
4. Roll or pull the dough into a large rectangular shape, 60cm (2 ft) long by 30cm (1ft) wide. Sprinkle over the gibbons and parsley and roll up from the long sides like a Swiss roll.
5. With a sharp knife cut the dough into sections or buns and stand them up on end.
6. Butter a baking sheet and place the buns fairly close together, so that they will touch when risen. Leave them to prove in a warm place for 30 minutes.
7. Brush the tops with milk and bake for 15 minutes in a hot oven.

Teisen Lap
(Moist Cake)

225g (8oz) plain flour
1 teaspoon baking powder
a pinch of salt
a pinch of grated nutmeg
100g (4oz) Welsh butter
75g (3oz) caster sugar
100g (4oz) sultanas
2 eggs, size 3, beaten
150m (1 ½ pint) buttermilk
  (or full fat milk + a good
  squeeze of lemon juice)

1. Sieve the flour, baking powder, salt and nutmeg
   into a bowl. Rub in the butter, and then add the
   sugar, fruit and eggs.
2. Add the buttermilk gradually, beating with a
   wooden spoon, until you have a mixture soft
   enough to drop, albeit reluctantly from the spoon.
3. Bake in a greased and lined 22cm (9") round
   sponge tin at 180°c, Gas mark 4, for 30–40
   minutes until golden brown and well risen.

Pikelets

300ml (½ pint) milk
2 eggs
75g (3 oz) butter, melted
100g (4 oz) flour
2 tablespoons currants, sultanas or raisins

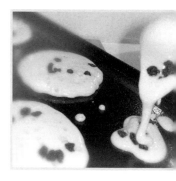

1. In a liquidiser or food processor, blend the milk, eggs, melted butter and flour into a smooth batter. Add the currants and leave to stand for 30 minutes.
2. Heat and lightly grease a griddle or heavy-based frying pan and bake one large ladleful or small cupful of the batter at a time until bubbles appear on the surface, then turn over and cook for another minute.
3. Serve hot and buttered with a sprinkling of sugar on top.

Summer

Come ye thankful people come
Raise the song of harvest home
All is safely gathered in
Ere the winter storms begin

Once summer is here, with the warmer weather and longer days, the crops grow like crazy and all this energy culminates in the harvest, whether it is in the back garden or out in the fields.

The very best flavours are here to enjoy in the summer. This is the time when fruit is ripened naturally in the sun, giving it the very best flavour.

Soups and Starters
Cream of Sorrel Soup
Cawl suran

50g (2oz) butter
1 medium onion, finely chopped
1 large potato, peeled and diced
2 good handfuls of freshly picked sorrel
600 ml (1 pint) milk
600 ml (1 pint) light chicken
   or vegetable stock
salt and freshly ground black pepper
lemon juice to taste

To garnish
A good dollop of cream

1. In a large saucepan, melt the butter and cook the onion and potato for 5 minutes over gentle heat. Toss in the sorrel leaves, stir for one minute, and then pour in all the liquid. Season well and bring to the boil.
2. Simmer the soup for 20 minutes then cool slightly before liquidizing or processing to a smooth puree.
3. Taste the soup carefully before adding lemon juice to sharpen the flavour and more seasoning if necessary. Reheat, and garnish with a swirl of cream just before serving.

Cream of Mushroom and Wild Garlic Soup

Dressed Crab with Fresh Herb Mayonnaise

1 teaspoon salt
4 live cock crabs, each weighing
    about 675g (1½ lbs)

fresh herb mayonnaise
2 egg yolks or 1 whole egg
300ml (½ pint) best quality olive oil
1 tablespoon white wine or cider vinegar

3 good handfuls of chopped
    fresh herbs (ideally sorrel,
    dill, chives, marjoram,
    basil and parsley)

garnish
paprika
4 sprigs parsley
4 wedges of lemon

To make the mayonnaise

1. Whisk the 2 egg yolks together in a small bowl, continue whisking and add the oil very, very slowly, until you have a thick emulsion. Add the vinegar to thin the mayonnaise to the right consistency, and then add a pinch of salt and the herbs. Alternatively, you can make mayonnaise in a liquidiser. Put the vinegar, whole egg and salt into the machine. With the motor running, gradually add the oil through the hole in the top until you have a thick emulsion.

To cook the crabs

2. Bring a very large pan of water to the boil Add the salt, then the crabs. Put the lid on the pan to bring the water back to boiling, and then simmer for 5 minutes. Turn off the heat and leave the crabs in the pot for another 10 minutes before removing and cooling quickly under the cold tap.

To dress the crabs

3. Working with 1 crab at a time, pull off the legs and prise the body from the under shell with the

point of a knife. Remove the inedible 'dead men's fingers' – the feathery looking gills at each side of the body, about a dozen in all.

4. Using as thin an instrument as you can find (ideally a crab pick but a crochet hook or knitting needle will work well), pick out all the white crab meat. Take out the stomach sac and discard. Scrape out the brown meat around the inside of the shell. Either pick out the legs and claws yourself, or crack them and let the diners do it themselves.

5. Wash the crab shells and pile the meat back in, with the brown meat at the sides and the white down the middle.

6. Garnish each dressed crab with a dusting of paprika, a sprig of parsley and a wedge of lemon. Serve with fresh herb mayonnaise, handed separately.

Deep Fried Cockles

225g (8oz) freshly boiled cockles, out of shell
225g (8oz) plain flour

salt and freshly ground black pepper
parsley sprigs

1. Squeeze excess moisture out of the cockles.
2. Put the flour in a bowl, season well and then add the cockles. Toss well to cover and then shake off excess flour.
3. Deep fry the cockles in moderately hot oil for 5 minutes until crisp.
4. Serve the cockles either in a small bowl as a nibble or as garnish for first course and main course dishes.
5. Garnish with deep fried parsley and serve with a flavoured mayonnaise.

33

Warm Quail's Egg and Cockle Salad

6 quail's eggs
175g (6oz) cockles, cooked
100g (4oz) Carmarthen ham
   or similar (Parma or Serrano)
50g (2oz) walnuts, broken into pieces
4 tablespoons walnut oil
2 tablespoons cider or white wine
   vinegar
salt and freshly ground black pepper
mixed salad leaves

1. Boil the quail's eggs by covering them with cold water in a pan and bringing up to the boil. Turn the heat down and simmer for 1 minute. Cool under the cold tap then peel.
2. Arrange the salad leaves on four plates.
3. In a large frying pan or skillet, heat the walnut oil and fry the mushrooms for one minute. Then toss in the cockles, ham and nuts and continue to fry, stirring all the time, for another minute.
4. Add the vinegar and seasoning and immediately pour the contents of the pan over the four plates of salad leaves, dividing the sauce evenly.
5. Cut the eggs in half and arrange over the salad.
6. Serve at once with warm rolls.

Baked Eggs with Bacon and Laver bread

4 fresh free range or organic eggs
4 tablespoons of laver bread seaweed
8 rashers of streaky bacon, grilled
    until crisp and cut into small dice
50g (2oz) butter
salt and pepper

1. Rub the butter around the sides and bottom of individual ramekin dishes. Sprinkle with seasoning.
2. Put a tablespoon of laver bread at the bottom of each ramekin with the bacon, saving some for decoration.
3. Break an egg into each dish, top with an egg yolk and a knob of butter.
4. Cover the dish with kitchen foil to prevent the surface drying in the heat.
5. Bake at 150°c/Gas mark 2 for 8–10 minutes, depending on the firmness required. Test by gently shaking the ramekins.
6. Decorate with the rest of the bacon.

35

Deep Fried Fingers of Plaice with Laver bread and Caper Mayonnaise

4 x 75g (3oz) plaice fillets cut
   into fingers
2 lemon wedges
2 sprigs of parsley
50g (2oz) flour
I egg beaten with a little milk
50g (2oz) breadcrumbs

Laver bread Seaweed and
   Caper Mayonnaise
Mix I tablespoon of laver bread and
I tablespoon chopped capers with
225g (8 ozs) mayonnaise.

1. One at a time, lightly coat the fingers
   of plaice with the flour, beaten egg and
   breadcrumbs. Shake off any excess.
2. Roll each lightly between the palms
   of your hands to neaten the shape.
3. Place them into a frying basket, then deep fry
   at 185C until crisp and golden brown (about 2 minutes).
4. Drain well and place in a warm serving dish. Decorate with
   the lemon wedges and plain parsley (or deep fried). Do not cover.
5. Serve at once, accompanied with the Laver bread and Caper
   Mayonnaise.

Fish and Shellfish
Seafood Kebabs
with Lime Dill Butter

8 large prawns
650g (1½ lbs) firm white fish,
   like monkfish, or cod
4 limes
1 small green chilli, de-seeded
   and finely chopped
2 tablespoons olive oil
salt and freshly ground black pepper

Lime Dill Butter
2 egg yolks
grated rind and juice of 1 lime
100g (4oz) butter
2 tablespoons chopped dill

1. Take 2 of the limes, grate the rind and squeeze the juice, put into a dish with the chilli and oil and season with salt and pepper.
2. Skin, bone and cut the white fish into 2.5 cm (1") cubes and put into the dish with the prawns, toss in the marinade then cover and refrigerate for 1 hour.
3. Cut the remaining limes into wedges and arrange on skewers with the fish. Brush with oil and cook under a hot grill or over hot coals for 6–8 minutes, turning once and brushing with the marinade.

To make the lime dill butter

1. Put the egg yolks into a bowl and whisk in the lime rind and juice. Place over a pan of simmering water and gradually whisk in little pieces of the butter, continue to whisk until the sauce thickens.
2. Remove from the pan and add the dill. Serve while still warm with seafood kebabs.

Glamorgan Sausages (Selsig Morgannwg)

Grilled Mackerel with Lovage

Grilled Mackerel with Lovage and Cracked Wheat Salad

4 plump mackerel, about 20cm (8")
   long, cleaned
I lemon, squeezed juice
a good sprig of lovage for each fish
salt and freshly ground black pepper

Cracked Wheat Salad
175g (8oz) cracked wheat (sometimes
   called bulgur or pourgouri)
a good handful of flat leaf parsley,
   chopped finely
25g (1oz) fresh mint, chopped finely
2 lemons, squeezed juice
2 tablespoons olive oil
salt
freshly ground black pepper
4 spring onions, trimmed and diced

1. Fill the cavity of the mackerel with the sprig of lovage, and then arrange the fish in a grill pan. (You may have to cook 2 at a time if your grill pan is small).
2. Squeeze over the juice of the lemon and season well.
3. Preheat the grill to its hottest then cook the fish for about 4–5 minutes each side. The skin should be crisp while the flesh is tender and moist.

For the Cracked Wheat Salad
2. Cover the bulgar wheat with boiling water and leave for 20 minutes.
3. Mix the herbs in a salad bowl with the lemon juice, olive oil, seasoning and spring onions.
4. Drain the bulgur and sprinkle the grains into the salad bowl.
5. Toss the salad well before serving.

Escalopes of Salmon or Sewin (Welsh Sea Trout)

4 escalopes or steaks of salmon or
   sewin, each weighing 100–175g
   (4–6oz)
4 sprigs of feathery fennel
4 slices of lemon
4 squares of buttered foil

Cucumber Sauce
½ cucumber, grated, sprinkled with
   salt and left for 10 minutes
2 tablespoons mayonnaise
2 tablespoons Greek-style yoghurt

1. Place an escalope of sewin on some buttered foil, lay a sprig of fennel and a slice of lemon on top and fold and seal the foil to make a parcel. Chill until ready to bake.
2. Preheat the oven to 200°c, Gas mark 6. Bake the fish for 8–10 minutes, or until the flesh has turned opaque.
3. Mix all the ingredients for the sauce.
4. Serve the fish escalopes in their foil wrapping with the sauce served separately.

Meat, Poultry and Offal
Rack of Welsh Lamb with Lavender Crust

1 teaspoon fresh lavender
   (or substitute rosemary)
75g (3oz) garlic-flavoured
   cream cheese
50g (2oz) fresh brown breadcrumbs
675–900g (1½–2lb) best end of neck
   of lamb, skinned and chined

1. Chop the lavender finely or grind it to a powder, and mix with the cream cheese and breadcrumbs. Press this mixture together with a palette knife and spread over the fat side of the lamb.
2. Put the rack of lamb in a roasting tin and cook in a hot oven 220°c, Gas mark 7, for 30 minutes, or a little longer if you do not like your lamb pink.
3. Serve the lamb, cut down between the rib bones, either as single cutlet or doubles. The meat will be deliciously juicy and the lavender crust will give a crisp outside to each cutlet.

No sauce is necessary; simply serve a moist vegetable dish such as carrot and leek medley.

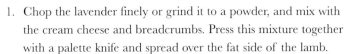

Spareribs in Honey

4 tablespoons clear honey
1 tablespoon soy sauce
3 tablespoons tomato ketchup
few drops Tabasco sauce
1 clove garlic, crushed with salt
salt to taste
1 teaspoon paprika
1 teaspoon mustard powder
juice and rind of 1 orange
4 tablespoons wine vinegar
300ml (½ pint) water, or water
   and white wine mixed
900g (2lb) Chinese-style (skinny)
   pork ribs

To garnish
12 Chinese spring onions

1. Mix the honey, soy sauce, tomato ketchup and Tabasco sauce in a bowl. Add garlic and season to taste with salt, paprika and mustard. Add grated orange rind, juice, wine vinegar and water.

2. Separate the ribs and soak in the sauce for at least 20 minutes in the fridge, turning from time to time.

3. Transfer the ribs and sauce to a large, oiled baking tray and bake in a hot oven (220°c, Gas mark 7) for about 40 minutes, turning from time to time so that no rib burns, but all brown evenly.

4. Either serve the glistening ribs straight from the oven on a large serving dish with the sauce poured over them, or finish off the cooking on a barbecue, to add the final crisp coating, and hand the sauce separately.

5. Garnish with Chinese spring onions and serve without cutlery. This is definitely a fingers-only meal. In fact, it might be a good idea to provide finger bowls.

6. For the Chinese spring onions – peel, top and tail them as usual then cut into each end to a depth of 5 cm (2in) like the end of a party cracker. Soak in iced water for about 10 minutes so that the ends fan out into attractive curls.

Breast of Chicken filled with Y Fenni Cheese

4 good sized chicken breasts,
   skin and bones removed
50g (2oz) Y Fenni cheese (substitute
   with cheddar and a teaspoon of
   wholegrain mustard)
1 tablespoon parsley, finely chopped
4 rashers streaky bacon, rind removed
25g (1oz) butter
juice of ½ lemon

1. Cut a slit in the side of each chicken
   breast and stuff with a slice of cheese
   and some parsley.
2. Wrap a rasher of bacon around each breast
   and pack the chicken pieces close together
   in a baking tin or open casserole.
3. Bake in a hot oven, 200°c, Gas mark 6, for
   20 minutes, or until the bacon is crisp and
   the chicken cooked right through.
4. Heat the butter in a small saucepan and
   when it starts to sizzle add the lemon juice.
5. Pour over the finished chicken.

Roast Pembrokeshire Duck with Whinberry Sauce

I large duck
salt and freshly ground
    black pepper
25g (1oz) butter

For the sauce
225g (8oz) whinberries
2 tablespoons redcurrant jelly
juice of I orange
100ml (4 fl oz) red wine
3 cardamom pods

1. Sprinkle the duck with pepper and salt and spread the butter over the breast. Roast in a hot oven, 220°c, Gas mark 7, allowing 15 minutes a pound of the trussed bird's weight. Baste frequently to obtain a good crisp skin.

2. To make the sauce, pick over the whinberries then cover with cold water in a small pan. Simmer until soft, about 5 minutes, and then add the redcurrant jelly, orange juice, red wine and ground seeds from the cardamom pods and simmer for another 5 minutes.

3. Liquidise or sieve the sauce, pressing the berries with the back of a wooden spoon to extract all the flavour.

4. To carve the duck, cut the crackling skin with the point of a sharp knife and cut the meat from the breast in thin, long slivers along the bone. To find the wing joints is no easy task: use carving secateurs or scissors, to save time and temper. Serve the duck with the sauce handed separately.

Roast Pembrokeshire Duck

43

Pan-fried Calves' Liver and Bacon

½ litre (1.1 pint) dark meat stock,
   reduced by two thirds
12 rashers rindless streaky bacon,
   thinly sliced
4 x 150g (6oz) slices calves' liver
good quality vegetable oil for frying
10g (1tsp) fresh sage
675g (1½ lbs) potatoes, boiled
   and mashed

1. Reduce the meat stock until it has thickened to a gravy-like consistency.
2. Crisp the bacon under a hot grill.
3. Pan-fry the calves' liver in a very hot pan with a little oil for 2–3 minutes on each side and leaving the middle slightly pink.
4. Deep-fry the sage leaves until crispy.
5. To serve: pile some mashed potatoes into the centre of a plate. Top first with the calves' liver, then the crisp bacon, and finally, the deep-fried sage leaves. Spoon some of the reduced sauce around.

Vegetables
Broad Beans in Sour Cream *(Ffa mewn hufen sur)*

450g (1lb) broad beans
(shelled weight)
150 ml (5 fl oz) sour cream
salt and freshly ground black pepper
grated nutmeg
½ teaspoon caraway or dill seeds
50g (2oz) butter
50g (2oz) fresh white breadcrumbs

1. Blanch the beans by cooking them in boiling water for 2 minutes then refreshing immediately under the cold tap.

2. Mix the sour cream with the salt, pepper, nutmeg and caraway seeds. Add the beans and transfer to a heatproof dish.

3. Melt the butter, stir in the breadcrumbs and arrange over the beans. Bake in a moderate oven, 180°c, Gas mark 4, for 15–20 minutes or until the topping is crisp and brown.

12 courgette flowers
4 sprigs of fresh basil, to garnish

For the tomato sauce
450g (1 lb) ripe tomatoes,
    roughly chopped
150ml (½ pint) water
pinch of cayenne pepper
40g (1½ oz) sun-dried tomatoes
sea salt and freshly ground black pepper

For the stuffing
1 small onion, finely chopped
1 celery stick, strings removed
    and finely chopped
15 g (½ oz) butter
25g (1 oz) toasted shelled hazelnuts
50g (2oz) pine nuts
100g (4 oz) fresh white breadcrumbs
1 egg, beaten
15 ml (1 tablespoon) chopped fresh basil

Stuffed Courgette Flowers

1. First make the tomato sauce: combine the tomatoes and water in a medium saucepan and bring to the boil. Turn down the heat and cook, covered, until the tomatoes have broken down. Add the cayenne pepper and sun-dried tomatoes and cook for another 5 minutes. Leave the sauce to cool a little before liquidising. Sieve, and then season to taste.

2. Make the stuffing: fry the onion and celery in the butter until soft. Mix with the remaining stuffing ingredients, then divide the mixture into 12 equal portions and form into sausage shapes.

3. Carefully press a portion of stuffing into each courgette flower, and then press the petals around the stuffing. Place the courgette flowers close together in a steamer and steam for 8–10 minutes.

4. Gently reheat the tomato sauce and spoon over individual plates. Top each serving with 3 courgette flowers and garnish with a sprig of fresh basil. Serve immediately.

Barbecued Corn on the Cob

4 corn on the cob
oil for brushing
salt and pepper
butter for serving

1. Strip corn cobs of leaves
   and fibres and wash.
2. Dry and brush with oil
   and season.
3. Put whole corn onto barbecue
   and turn occasionally until the
   corn is golden brown all over.
4. Serve hot with butter.

Green Salad with Honey Dressing
(Salad Gwyrdd gyda Mêl)

1 crisp lettuce – an iceberg,
   Webb's Wonder or cos
1 bunch watercress
2 tablespoons fresh parsley, chopped
2 tablespoons fresh chervil, basil
   or sage chopped
2 tablespoons fresh rosemary,
   thyme or savory, chopped
a few edible flowers (optional)

For the honey dressing
6 tablespoons best quality olive oil
2 tablespoons cider vinegar or lemon juice
1 teaspoon honey
1 teaspoon wholegrain mustard
salt and freshly ground black pepper

1. Rinse and dry all the salad ingredients. Shred the lettuce.

2. In a large salad bowl combine the lettuce with the watercress and freshly chopped herbs. Sprinkle the flowers over the top.

3. Combine all the ingredients for the dressing in a screw-topped jar. Shake well and pour over the salad just before serving. Toss well.

Desserts
Whisked Sponge with Strawberries and Elderflower

*Makes 15cm (6")
sandwich cake*

2 eggs
50g (2oz) caster sugar
50g (2oz) plain flour, sieved twice
$\frac{1}{2}$ vanilla essence

Filling and Topping
225 (8oz) fresh strawberries,
   sliced + 5 small ones for garnish
2 tablespoons elderflower cordial
300ml ($\frac{1}{2}$ pint) double cream

1. Very lightly grease and line the base and sides of two 15 cm (6") sandwich tins.
2. Whisk the eggs and sugar in a bowl using an electric mixer for 5 to 10 minutes or until the mixture is light in colour and very thick. It increases in volume by about two thirds. When the whisk is lifted up it should leave a trail in the mixture for at least 5 seconds. (If whisking by hand, sit the bowl over a pan of hot water to speed up the process.)
3. With a large metal spoon, fold the flour and essence into the mixture, cutting and folding until all the flour is incorporated.
4. Divide the mixture evenly into the sandwich tins.
5. Spread with a palette knife to level the mixture in the tins before baking at 180°c, Gas mark 4, for 20–25 minutes or until well risen and golden brown.

6. When cooled a little, turn out the cakes on to a wire cooling tray.
7. Just before filling, peel off the lining paper.

For the filling and topping

1. Macerate the sliced strawberries in the elderflower cordial for an hour.
2. Whisk the cream till thick but not stiff.
3. Mix ½ of the cream with the strawberries and use this as filling between the two sponges.
4. Pipe the remaining cream into 5 swirls on the top of the cake and decorate with the remaining strawberries.

Sponge with Strawberries and Elderflower

Whinberry Pie

Whinberry Pie

For the Pastry
350g (12oz) plain flour
175g (6oz) butter and lard,
   mixed
100g (4oz) caster sugar
1 egg yolk
a few tablespoons cold
   water to mix

For the Filling
450g (1lb) fresh whinberries,
   picked over
5 large cooking apples
75g (3oz) caster sugar
pinch of cinnamon
juice of half a lemon
caster sugar to glaze

For the Pastry

1. Rub the fat into the flour until it looks like breadcrumbs then stir in the sugar.
2. Add the egg yolk and enough cold water to make a firm dough.
3. Cover and leave to rest in the fridge.

For the Filling

1. Peel and slice the cooking apples and cook in a saucepan with the sugar, cinnamon and lemon juice. (The apples should be soft but not lose their shape or mush to a puree). Leave to cool.
2. Roll the pastry out to line an 8" flan tin, reserving about a third for the pie lid.
3. Spoon in layers of the apples and whinberries.
4. Cover the pie with the lid, brush with cold water and sprinkle with sugar.
5. Bake at 190°c, Gas mark 5, for 25 minutes or until golden brown.
6. Serve with fresh cream or a light custard.

Flummery with Oatmeal,
Summer Fruits and Yoghurt

100g (4oz) medium oatmeal
1 tablespoon heather honey
1 tablespoon caster sugar
1 tablespoon fresh lemon juice
225g (8oz) summer fruit, such as
   strawberries or raspberries
300ml (½ pint) Greek-style yoghurt

1. Soak all but a spoonful of the oatmeal in cold water
    overnight. The oatmeal will absorb about twice its
    volume in water.
2. Next day, strain off any excess water. Place the creamy
    oatmeal into a bowl and stir in the honey, caster sugar
    and lemon juice. Add the yoghurt and taste for sweetness.
3. Chop the fruit into bite-sized pieces and arrange in the
    bottom of one large or six individual glass dishes. Spoon
    over the oatmeal cream.
4. Toast the remaining oatmeal until brown and nutty,
    either in a dry frying pan or under the grill, or bake in
    the oven for 10 minutes. Sprinkle a dusting of toasted
    oatmeal on top.

Strawberry and Elderflower Tartlets

Strawberry and Elderflower Tartlets

125g (4½ oz) unsalted butter
75g (3oz) icing sugar
1 egg yolk
1 whole egg
250g (9oz) plain flour

For the Filling
450g (1lb) fresh strawberries
3 tablespoons redcurrant jelly
3 tablespoons elderflower cordial

1. First make the pastry: cream the butter with the icing sugar until very pale, then add the egg yolk and whole egg and beat hard.
2. Fold in the flour and mix to a firm paste. Cover and chill in the refrigerator for 30 minutes.
3. Roll out the pastry thinly and, using a fluted pastry cutter, line 10–12 tartlet tins. Leave to rest for 10 minutes.
4. Bake blind at 200°c, Gas mark 6, for 10 to 15 minutes until lightly coloured.
5. Leave to cool on a rack.
6. Hull the strawberries and cut the larger ones into quarters.
7. In a small pan, blend the redcurrant jelly with the elderflower cordial and heat gently, stirring all the time until the mixture is smooth.
8. Arrange the strawberries in the tartlets, and brush with the redcurrant jelly to glaze.
9. Decorate with elderflower blossom in season (May/June)

Baking
Pastai Pen y Fan

675g (1½lb) pizza dough mix

Make up the pizza dough mix according to instructions on the packet.

Filling
1 tablespoon olive oil
25g (1oz) butter
1 carrot, peeled and diced
1 parsnip, peeled and diced
½ onion or a small leek, diced
2 tablespoons cabbage, diced
2 tablespoons parsley, chopped
175g–225g (6–8oz) smoked collar
   of bacon, cooked and diced
50g (2oz) St Illtyd cheese (cheddar
   with garlic, wine and herbs)

For the filling
1. Heat the oil and butter and fry all the vegetables together very gently until soft. Add the bacon and cheese and leave to cool.
2. Roll the dough into 12 small balls then flatten out into six inch discs.
3. Place two tablespoons of the filling on each disc, and fold the dough over to cover.
4. Seal the edges of the dough with egg wash and also brush the pasty.
5. Leave the pasties to rise for 15 minutes then cook in a hot oven 215°c, Gas mark 7, for 20 minutes, until golden brown.

Caerphilly Scones

Caerphilly Scones

225g (8oz) wholemeal self-raising flour
salt and cayenne pepper
35g (1½ oz) butter
50g (2oz) Caerphilly cheese, grated
1 teaspoon caster sugar
150ml (½ pint) milk, plus milk to glaze

1. Mix the seasoning into the flour then rub in the butter. Add the cheese and sugar and enough milk to make a soft but manageable dough.
2. Turn on to a floured board, knead as quickly and lightly as possible and pat the dough out to about 4cm (1½") thick.
3. Shape into scones with a knife or pastry cutter and place on a greased baking sheet.
4. Brush with milk and bake in a hot oven 220°c, Gas mark 7, for 10 minutes.
5. Serve hot from the oven, well-buttered.

Shell Shortbread –
Teisen Beffro

Makes 25–30

175g (6oz) Welsh butter
225g (8oz) plain flour
100g (4oz) caster sugar,
    plus extra for dredging

1. Rub the butter into the flour until the mixture resembles fine breadcrumbs. Stir in the sugar.
2. Using your fingertips, press the mixture together and knead to a smooth pliable paste. Roll out fairly thinly on a well-floured board and cut into 5 cm (2") circles. Using the tip of a sharp-bladed knife mark each with a scallop shell pattern.
3. Bake in a moderately hot oven 190°c, Gas 5, for about 10 minutes until the biscuits turn a pale golden colour.
4. Cool on a baking tray and when cold sprinkle lavishly with caster sugar. Store in an airtight tin for up to a week.

Autumn

Miller, o miller, o dusty-poll,
How many sacks of flour hast thou stole?
In goes a bushel, out comes a peck,
Hang old Miller-Dee up by the neck

In the past, autumn was the busiest season in the kitchen; the time of year to gather, salt, cure, pickle or bottle all good ingredients ready for the winter. Time hardly allows us to make such preparations these days, but how satisfying it is to set a pan of chutney on the stove to boil and enjoy the pungency of the boiling vinegar.

At least we should be able to find the time to scour some hedgerows for delicious, juicy brambles to add that special flavour to pies and crumbles.

Bacon Cawl
with Vegetables

1kg (2lbs) piece of bacon or gammon,
   shoulder or corner
1 onion cut in half
1 carrot
1 parsnip
1 bay leaf
a bunch of parsley, stems and tops
   used separately
1 large leek, white and green part
   separated and diced
3 carrots, peeled and cubed
2 parsnips, peeled and cubed
2 turnips, peeled and cubed
25g (1oz) butter
a bunch of fresh winter savory or sage
salt and pepper

1. Soak the bacon or gammon overnight in cold water to remove some
    of the salt. Rinse well and place in a large pan with enough cold
    water to cover. Add the onion, carrot, parsnip, bay leaf and parsley
    stalks. Simmer gently for an hour, then leave to cool before skimming
    the fat from the surface.

2. Remove the bacon from the stock, strain the liquor and retain
    for later. Remove some bacon slices and set aside for another meal,
    before cutting the remainder into chunks for the cawl.

3. Gently fry the cubed carrots, parsnips, turnips and the white portion
    of the leek in the butter. Pour on the reserved stock; add the chunks
    of bacon and the chopped parsley, savory and green leek. Simmer
    for a further 20 minutes. Season well.

4. Serve the cawl with chunks of fresh bread. Alternatively, leave
    overnight for the flavours to develop.

Cream of Mushroom and Wild Garlic Soup

450g (1lb) fresh mushrooms,
    cleaned and sliced
50g (2oz) butter
1 teaspoon oil
1 small onion, peeled and chopped
2 celery sticks, cleaned and chopped
1 small leek, cleaned and chopped
50g (2oz) plain flour
1.2l (2 pints) good vegetable stock
300ml (½ pint) milk
1 dessertspoon fresh thyme, chopped
1 dessertspoon fresh tarragon, chopped
salt and pepper
swirl of cream to serve
croutons
wild garlic (ramsons) to garnish

1. Melt the butter and oil in a heavy based saucepan. Gently fry the onion, celery and leek until softened.
2. Add the flour and cook, stirring with a wooden spoon, for a minute.
3. Gradually stir in the stock and bring up to the boil.
4. Add the mushrooms and herbs and simmer gently for 30 minutes, stirring occasionally.
5. Add the milk and, when cool enough, liquidise to a smooth puree.
6. When ready to serve, warm through in a clean pan and season to taste.
7. Serve in warmed bowls garnished with croutons and a swirl of cream and chopped fresh wild garlic.

Glamorgan Sausages
(Selsig Morgannwg)

150g (5oz) fresh breadcrumbs
1 small leek, washed and very
    finely chopped
75g (3oz) Caerphilly cheese, grated
1 tablespoon fresh parsley, chopped
salt and freshly ground black pepper
pinch of dry mustard
3 medium eggs
oil or bacon fat (for non-vegetarians)
    for frying

To garnish
Sprigs of fresh parsley

1. Mix together the breadcrumbs, leek, cheese, parsley, seasonings and mustard.
2. Beat the eggs together and stir in to bind the mixture. Divide into 12 portions and form into sausage shapes. Chill for 20 minutes.
3. Fry gently in oil or bacon fat until crisp and golden brown on all sides. Serve immediately, with fruity autumn chutney, garnished with fresh parsley.

Autumn Chutney

I large onion, peeled and chopped
I clove garlic, chopped
I x I" chunk of fresh ginger,
   peeled and grated
I teaspoon ground cinnamon
450g (Ilb) cooking apples, peeled,
   cored and chopped
450g (Ilb) pears, peeled, cored
   and chopped
450g (Ilb) plums, stoned and chopped
375g (I2oz) Demerara sugar
2–3 tablespoons cider vinegar
2–3 tablespoons water
225g (8oz) mixed dried fruit

1. In a large saucepan combine the onion, garlic, ginger, cinnamon, apples, pears, plums, sugar, vinegar and water. Bring to the boil
   and then stew gently for about 45 minutes.
2. Leave to cool then puree the mixture in a processor.
3. Add the dried fruit when the mixture is completely cool.

Prawn, Leek and Caerphilly Cheese Bake

24 large prawns or tiger prawns,
    shell on, uncooked
1 leek, washed and diced
25g (1oz) butter
150ml (½) pint double cream
100g (4 oz) Caerphilly cheese, grated
pinch of nutmeg
salt and freshly ground black pepper
50g (2oz) fresh brown breadcrumbs

1. Steam the prawns for 2–3 minutes, until they have turned pink. Cool immediately under the cold tap and remove the shells.
2. Cook the leek gently in the butter till soft.
3. Arrange the leek in the bottom of 4 individual serving dishes, with 6 prawns on top.
4. Mix the cream with the cheese, nutmeg and seasoning and pour over the prawns.
5. Sprinkle over the breadcrumbs
6. Bake in a hot oven or pop under a moderate grill for 10 minutes until bubbling and golden brown on top.

Warm Salad of Pigeon Breast with Walnuts

4 rashers of streaky bacon, diced
100g (4oz) field mushrooms
12 walnuts, shelled
2 pigeon breast cut into slivers
1 dessertspoon cider vinegar
2 tablespoons walnut oil
a selection of salad leaves
chopped parsley to garnish

1. Arrange the clean, dry salad leaves on four individual plates. In a large, heavy-based frying pan, gently dry-fry the bacon until the fat runs. Add the mushrooms and allow them to absorb the bacon fat. Add the walnuts and turn up the heat, stirring all the time.

2. Add half the oil, toss in the slivers of pigeon breast, stir over brisk heat, to seal on all sides, and cook thoroughly.

3. Scatter the pigeon, bacon, mushrooms and walnuts over the lettuce and deglaze the pan with the cider vinegar, heating gently and stirring to collect the juices.

4. Take the pan off the heat, add the remaining oil, blend well and pour at once over the salads.

5. Garnish with chopped parsley and serve at once with walnut and herb rolls.

Grilled Bacon and Laver bread Rolls

1. In a bowl, mix the laver bread and oatmeal together to make a stiff paste, season well with freshly ground black pepper. Divide into 12 portions.
2. Wrap a rasher of bacon around each portion of laver bread and oatmeal to make a bacon roll. Secure with a cocktail stick if necessary.
3. Grill, turning from time to time until the bacon is crisp.
4. Serve with breakfast or as part of a main meal.

12 rashers smoked streaky bacon
100g (4oz) laver bread seaweed,
  fresh or tinned
25g (1oz) pinhead or medium oatmeal
freshly ground black pepper

Fillet of Salmon cooked in paper with Lady Llanover's Granville Sauce

4 x 275g (6oz) fillets of salmon
1 leek, finely chopped
salt and pepper
greaseproof paper

Lady Llanover's
  Granville Sauce
1 small anchovy, pounded
  in a mortar
1 shallot, finely chopped
2 tablespoons dry sherry
half a tablespoon best vinegar
6 whole peppercorns
a little nutmeg
a very little mace
6 tablespoons of cream

1. Place a salmon fillet or portion in the centre of a circle of greaseproof paper. Tuck some leeks under the fish, and scatter a few on top. Season well.
2. Wrap the paper over the fish in order to seal it, and then bake in a medium oven for about 8–10 minutes.

Lady Llanover's Granville Sauce

1. Simmer all the ingredients for the sauce, except the cream, very gently, stirring well all the time, until the shallot is soft.
2. Place half an ounce of butter in another saucepan, with as much flour as will make it into a stiff paste. Add the other ingredients, which have been simmering, and stir well, till scalding hot, for about 2 minutes. Add the cream, stir well and strain.
3. Serve the salmon either in or out of the paper, with a garnish of leek and a little of the sauce.

Baked Trout in Bacon

4 good sized trout
1 tablespoon chopped chives
4 slices of lemon
salt and freshly ground black pepper
8 rashers smoked streaky bacon

Horseradish sauce
Greek yogurt mixed with a little
   freshly grated horseradish
   and chopped parsley

1. Pre-heat the oven to 200°c, Gas mark 6.
2. Clean, gut and, if possible, bone the trout. (The best way to do this is to open up the trout, spread it tummy down on a board and press hard along the back – this loosens the bones from the flesh. Then, starting at the head end, ease away the backbone with the tip of a knife, removing at the same time as many of the small bones as possible).
3. Place some chopped chives and a slice of lemon in the belly of each fish, and season with salt and pepper.
4. Wrap each fish in two rashers of bacon and lay them side by side in a baking dish. Bake for 15–20 minutes, until the bacon is crisp on top and the trout flesh is cooked and flaky.
5. Serve with horseradish sauce.

65

Potted Trout

450g (1lb) trout fillets, skinned
1 tablespoon chopped dill
1 teaspoon ground mace
salt and freshly-ground black pepper
225g (8oz) slightly salted creamy butter

1. Preheat the oven to 180°c, Gas mark 4.
2. Remove any small bones from the fish fillets and arrange half in one layer in a small earthenware pot or terrine. Sprinkle the chopped dill, ground mace and seasoning over the fish and arrange the remaining fillets on top.
3. In a small pan, heat the butter gently without boiling. The creamy sediment will gather in the bottom of the pan so pour the clarified butter from the top carefully over the fish fillets so that they are completely covered.
4. Garnish with a sprig of dill and cover the pot with foil or a lid and bake in the oven for 20 minutes.
5. Chill in the fridge for at least four hours to let the butter harden before serving with crisp toast.

Meat, Poultry and Offal
Loin of Welsh Lamb with a Laver bread and Orange Stuffing

675–900g (1½ –2lb) loin of lamb,
    skinned and boned
seasoned flour
1 egg, beaten
fresh brown breadcrumbs
50g (2oz) lard or 1 tablespoon cooking oil

For the stuffing
1 rasher streaky bacon, chopped
1 medium onion, chopped
50g (2oz) laver bread (omit if you wish)
grated rind of ½ orange
salt and freshly ground black pepper

Loin of Welsh Lamb

For the sauce
25g (1oz) butter
1 small onion,
    finely diced
1 tablespoon flour
300ml (½ pint) good
    brown stock
1 teaspoon tomato puree
juice of ½ orange
3 tablespoons red wine
salt and freshly ground
    black pepper

1. To make the stuffing, dry-fry the bacon gently in a pan until the fat runs, add the onion and cook for a further 5 minutes until soft but not brown. Add the laver bread, grated orange rind and seasoning. Leave to cool.

2. Spread the stuffing down the centre of the loin, roll it up and, with a strong thread, sew loosely (so that the meat can expand during cooking) to form a long sausage shape.

3. Roll the loin in seasoned flour then brush with beaten egg and roll in the breadcrumbs, pressing them on with a palette knife so that the entire loin is covered.

4. In a moderately hot oven, 200°c, Gas mark 6, melt the dripping in a roasting pan and roast the loin for 1 hour, turning every 15 minutes so that it browns evenly on all sides.

5. Meanwhile, make the sauce: melt the butter and cook the onion over very gentle heat for 10 minutes. Stir in the flour and continue to cook gently until the flour has turned a good mid-brown colour. Gradually add the stock, tomato puree, orange juice and red wine. Season well and leave to simmer for 20 minutes. Strain and adjust seasoning before serving.

6. Leave the cooked loin to rest for 5 minutes, and then carefully pull out the thread. Serve the lamb carved into slices with the sauce passed separately.

Pan Fried Venison on a Leek and Potato Cake

4 venison loin steaks, about 175g
  (6 oz) each
1 glass red wine
1 teaspoon coriander seeds
½ orange, grated rind and juice
1 tablespoon redcurrant jelly
1 tablespoon olive oil
salt and freshly ground pepper
2 large potatoes, peeled
1 small leek, washed

1. Combine the wine, coriander seeds and orange rind with the oil and pour over the venison steaks. Leave to marinate for at least an hour before cooking.

2. To prepare the rosti, grate the potato and leek and mix together with seasoning. Divide into four. Fry over gentle heat, shaped into a disc in a metal pastry cutter. Turn once to cook both sides.

3. Drain the venison from the marinade and pat dry on kitchen paper. Fry briskly to seal on both sides then lower the heat and cook for another 4 minutes, until cooked but pink in the middle.

4. Dish a rosti onto each serving plate, slice the venison steaks and arrange on top and keep warm.

5. Add the marinade to the steak pan juices and stir well, then add the orange juice and redcurrant jelly and boil to reduce by half. Taste for seasoning and pour around the steaks.

Kidneys with Blackberry Mustard and Parsnip Pancake

12 Welsh lambs' kidneys
light vegetable oil for frying
2 shallots, finely chopped
1 glass dry sherry
200ml (7fl oz) lamb stock
2 tablespoons blackberry mustard
   (substitute wholegrain mustard)
salt and freshly ground black pepper
25g (1oz) butter
2 spring onions, chopped, for garnish
For the pancakes
300g (11oz) self-raising flour
300ml (½ pint) cold milk
2 eggs beaten
175g (6oz) cooked parsnip, cubed
6 spring onions, chopped

1. First make the pancakes by putting the flour into a bowl and whisking in the milk to make a smooth paste. Add the eggs, parsnip and spring onions then season well. The batter should be of nearly pouring texture.

2. Pour a little of light vegetable oil into a non-stick pan and spoon in a ¼ of batter mix. Cook on both sides until golden brown. Repeat so that you have 4 pancakes in all. Leave to drain on kitchen paper.

3. Skin, halve and core each kidney. Heat a tablespoon of oil in a large frying pan and quickly sauté the kidneys until they are just firm and lightly browned. (Do them in batches if you haven't got a large pan). Add the shallot and sherry and cook to reduce, then add the stock and mustard and simmer until the kidneys are just cooked. Do not overcook or they will become rubbery.

4. Arrange the kidneys on the hot pancakes on 4 warm plates. Reduce the sauce in the pan, season, add the butter and, when melted, pour over the kidneys. Garnish with chopped spring onion.

Baked Duck with Plums

Baked Duck with Plums

4 duck breasts
6–8 good sized plums
1–2 tablespoons balsamic vinegar
1 tablespoon honey
salt and pepper
pinch of cinnamon

1. Heat a heavy-based casserole dish and gently dry-fry the duck for about 5 minutes, breast-side down until the fat melts and the skin is golden brown.
2. Drain off excessive fat then add the vinegar, honey, fruit, spice and seasoning. Cover the pan and simmer very gently for 15–20 minutes.
3. Remove the duck and slice onto a serving dish. Drain off any remaining fat and reduce the juices until syrupy. Serve with the duck.

Braised Monmouthshire Pork with Savoury Welsh cakes

4 pork loin chops
salt and pepper
1 tablespoon oil
25g (1oz) butter
2 medium onions, peeled and sliced
2 cooking apples, peeled, cored and quartered
300ml (½ pint) cider
2 tablespoons soft brown sugar
1–2 teaspoons corn flour to thicken

Savoury Welsh cakes
225g (8oz) self-raising flour
100g (4oz) butter, cut into small pieces
1 tablespoon fresh chopped herbs
pinch dried mustard seasoning
1 egg, beaten
milk if necessary to mix

Braised Monmouthshire Pork

1. Heat the oil with the butter in a heavy-based casserole. Brown the chops quickly on both sides and remove.
2. Fry the onions until soft then add the apples, cider and sugar and return the chops to the casserole. Cook gently for 40 minutes at 180°c, Gas mark 4, or until the pork is tender.
3. To prepare the Savoury Welsh cakes, put the flour into a large bowl or food processor and add the butter. Rub or process until it looks like fine breadcrumbs. Add the herbs, mustard, seasoning and egg and enough milk to bind to a soft dough.
4. Roll the dough out to 1cm (½ ") thick and cut with a 5cm (2") cutter into discs. Griddle in a lightly greased pan to cook through from both sides.
5. Lift the pork chops out of the casserole, arrange on a serving dish, and scatter the apples and onions on top.
6. Reheat the sauce and adjust the consistency by thickening with corn flour that has been slaked with a little cold water. Boil until thickened and season if necessary. Pour the sauce over the pork and garnish the dish with the savoury Welsh cakes.

Stuffed Hearts

4 lambs' hearts
seasoned flour
50g (2oz) unsalted butter
450ml ($\frac{1}{2}$ pint) brown stock
1 large onion, peeled and chopped
225g (8oz) carrots, peeled and
    chopped
1 celery heart, chopped

Stuffing
1 leek, washed and chopped
1 stick celery, finely chopped
50g (2oz) bacon, diced small
50g (2oz) breadcrumbs, fresh white
1 tablespoon chopped parsley
1 tablespoon chopped fresh sage
grated rind of 1 lemon
salt and pepper
1 tablespoon honey
40g ($1\frac{1}{2}$ oz) melted butter

1. Prepare the stuffing; combine all the dry
   ingredients and bind with the honey and melted butter.
2. Rinse the hearts thoroughly under cold running water to
   remove all traces of blood.
3. Snip out the tubes with scissors and fill the hearts with the
   stuffing, be careful not to stuff the hearts too tightly, as the
   filling swells during cooking.
4. Sew up the opening and coat the hearts with seasoned flour.
5. Melt the butter in a heavy-based pan and fry the hearts over high
   heat, turning them until evenly browned. Lift the hearts into an
   ovenproof casserole dish.
6. Stir enough seasoned flour into the pan to absorb all the fat. Cook
   for a few minutes, then gradually stir in the stock and bring to the
   boil. Correct seasoning and pour the sauce over the hearts.

Carrot and Leek Medley

7. Cover the casserole with a lid and cook on the lowest shelf in a pre-heated oven at 170°c, Gas mark 3, for 2 hours.
8. Add the vegetables to the casserole and continue cooking, at the same temperature, for another hour.
9. Serve the hearts, vegetables and sauce straight from the casserole. Fluffy boiled rice or buttered noodles would go well with this substantial dish.

450g (1 lb) leeks, washed and finely chopped – choose slim young ones if possible
225g (½ lb) carrots, peeled and grated

salt and freshly ground black pepper
25g (1oz) butter
4 tablespoons water

1. Combine the vegetables in an ovenproof dish and season well. Cut the butter into slivers, distribute over the top and add the water.
2. Braise, covered, for 30 minutes in a moderate oven, 180°c, Gas mark 4, until the leeks and carrots are cooked but still just crunchy.
3. Fluff up the vegetables with a fork to lighten the texture and serve immediately, before they lose their bright colour.

N.B. Can be cooked in the microwave

Anglesey Eggs

Anglesey Eggs

450g (1lb) potatoes, peeled
salt and freshly ground black pepper
3 leeks, washed and chopped
50g (2oz) butter
50g (2oz) plain flour
600 ml (1 pint) milk
75g (3 oz) Caerphilly cheese, grated
4 eggs, hard-boiled and shelled

1. Boil the potatoes in salted water until soft.
2. Cook the leeks in salted water for 10 minutes, or add to the potatoes for the last 10 minutes of their cooking time.
3. Drain well then combine, season and mash together.
4. Make a cheese sauce. Melt the butter in a saucepan, stir in the flour and cook for a minute, then gradually stir in the milk and bring to the boil to thicken. Season well and add half of the cheese.
5. Take 4 individual dishes, or 1 family dish, and with a fork arrange the leek and potato mixture around the sides.
6. Slice the eggs in half and put an egg into each individual dish or all the eggs into the bigger dish. Cover with the cheese sauce and sprinkle over the remaining cheese.
7. Brown quickly under a hot grill or heat through in a very hot, preheated oven at 230°c, Gas 8, for 10 minutes.

For the batter
100g (4oz) flour
1 egg
1 yolk
300 ml (½ pint) liquid
    (almost all milk but add
    a dash of water)
1 tablespoon light cooking oil
2 tablespoons cooked spinach,
    chopped
salt and freshly ground
    black pepper

To garnish
25g (1oz) toasted pine nuts or sunflower seeds – to
toast, simply heat gently in a frying pan, in the oven,
or under a medium grill, until brown – this always
takes longer than you anticipate. Nuts brown well
in the microwave too; place them directly on the
turntable dish and stir from time to time.

For the filling
225g (8oz) low-fat curd cheese
225g (8oz) cooked spinach,
    chopped
25g (1oz) pine nuts
    or sunflower seeds
25g (1oz) fresh Parmesan
    cheese, grated
salt,
freshly ground black pepper,
freshly grated nutmeg

Spinach Pancakes
(Crempogau Pigoglys)

1. Put all the ingredients for the batter in a liquidiser
   or food processor and whiz until smooth.
2. For the filling, mix all the ingredients, blend
   together well.
3. In a lightly greased 20cm (8in) frying pan, fry thin
   pancakes and stack to keep them moist.
4. Spoon the filling into the pancakes, fold and
   arrange in a heatproof dish.
5. Bake in a hot oven, 220°c, Gas mark 7, for 15
   minutes, or put under a medium grill for 15 minutes.
6. Serve the pancakes piping hot with a crunchy
   garnish of toasted nuts or seeds scattered
   over the top.

Spinach Pancakes (Crempogau Pigoglys)

Mushrooms and Onions in a Cream Sauce

50g (2 oz) butter
1 large onion, chopped
4 sticks celery, chopped
450g (1lb) mushrooms, chopped
1 tablespoon plain flour
150ml (¼ pint) vegetable stock
½ teaspoon dried thyme
a small pinch of ground bay leaf
150 ml (¼ pint) double cream
lemon juice to taste
salt and freshly ground pepper

1. Melt half the butter in a saucepan and sauté the onion and celery gently until the onion is transparent.
2. Add the remaining butter and the mushrooms, and cook for 2–3 minutes over medium heat, stirring occasionally.
3. Stir in the flour, add the stock and herbs and bring to the boil. Reduce the heat and simmer for 2–3 minutes then take off the heat. Stir in the cream and lemon juice and season to taste.
4. Heat gently and serve with boiled rice, pasta or a jacket potato.

Sweet Marrow Pie

350g (12oz) prepared sweet short crust pastry
3 eggs
100g (4oz) caster sugar
100g (4oz) Demerara sugar
450g (1lb) marrow, peeled and seeded
1½ teaspoons ground cinnamon
1 teaspoon ground ginger
½ teaspoon mixed spice
½ teaspoon ground cloves
½ teaspoon ground cardamom
a pinch of salt
good ½ (300 ml) double cream
walnut halves to decorate

1. Line 2 x 8 inch (20cm) deep flan dishes with the pastry.
2. In a food processor, combine the eggs and sugar until smooth. Grate the marrow and add to the processor with all the spices and the cream. Process to mix well.
3. Pour into the prepared flan dish and decorate with walnut halves. Bake in a preheated oven at 230°c, Gas mark 8, for 8 minutes, then turn down to 170°c, Gas mark 3, and bake for a further 35 minutes, or until cooked, set and golden brown.

Blackberry Batter Pudding

4 whole eggs plus 2 yolks
25g (1oz) plain flour
50g (2oz) caster sugar
pinch of salt

1 pint milk
450g (1lb) fresh blackberries
2–3 tablespoons brandy
icing sugar

1. Butter a 10" ovenproof baking dish and arrange the berries over the base. In a liquidiser blend the whole eggs, yolks, flour, sugar, salt and milk until well mixed.
2. Pour the batter over the blackberries. Place the dish on a baking sheet.
3. Bake in the oven at 190°c, Gas mark 5, for 30–40 minutes, or until the batter is puffed up and golden brown.
4. Remove from the oven and allow to cool; the batter pudding may sink a little. Spoon over the brandy and dust with icing sugar before serving.

Autumn Fruit Brulée

2 large cooking apples, peeled, cored and chopped
2 ripe pears, peeled, cored and chopped
100g (4oz) blackberries
4 tablespoons water
100g (4oz) granulated sugar

Custard Mixture
4 large egg yolks
1 level tablespoon caster sugar
600ml (1pint) double cream
1 vanilla pod, split or a few drops of essence
caster sugar to cover

For the Custard

1. Mix the yolks well with the tablespoon of sugar.
2. Put the cream and vanilla pod together into a double saucepan. Cover and bring up to scalding point, then remove the pod and pour the cream on to the yolks, blending well.
3. Return the cream to the pan and thicken carefully over heat, stirring constantly. Don't let it boil.
4. Strain the cream over the ramekins of purée and chill in the fridge overnight.
5. Next day, sprinkle caster sugar evenly over the surface of the cream.
6. Heat the grill (or blow torch) and grill/glaze the top of the fruit brulée until the sugar has melted to a golden brown and the surface is hard to the touch.

For the Fruit Puree

1. Combine the prepared apples and pears with the water and poach, or microwave, over low heat until soft. Add the blackberries for the last 5 minutes of cooking.
2. Purée the fruit mixture and leave to cool.
3. Spread a layer of purée 1cm (½") thick in the bottoms of 6–8 small ramekin dishes.

Berry Lemon Pudding

225g (½ lb) blackberries, currants,
   whinberries, or any fresh fruit
   you have to hand
25g (1oz) unsalted butter
100g (4oz) soft brown sugar
grated rind and juice of 1 lemon
25g (1oz) flour
2 eggs separated
150ml (½ pint) milk

1. Prepare the fruit: wash and hull the berries, set a few aside for decoration and put the rest into a 600ml (1 pint) soufflé dish.
2. In a large bowl, cream together the butter with half of the sugar. Add the grated lemon rind then add alternately, beating hard between each addition, the remaining sugar, the flour, egg yolks and milk.
3. Whisk the egg whites till stiff and fold them into the mixture. Pour on to the fruit and sit the soufflé dish in a baking tin containing 2.5 cm (1inch) of water.
4. Cook in a moderate oven, 180°c, Gas mark 4, for 45 minutes, until the top is brown and spongy.
5. Serve hot, dredged with caster sugar, or cold, with a decoration of piped cream and the remaining berries.

Baking
Spiced Honey Buns

100g (4oz) butter
100g (4oz) soft brown sugar
1 egg, separated
100 ml (4fl oz) honey
225g (8oz) plain flour
$\frac{1}{2}$ teaspoon bicarbonate of soda
$\frac{1}{2}$ teaspoon ground cinnamon
1–2 tablespoons milk
caster sugar to dredge

1. Cream the butter and sugar together until light and fluffy – this process is important and, the longer you beat, the better the cakes will be. Add the egg yolk and honey.
2. Sieve together the flour, bicarbonate of soda and cinnamon and fold into the mixture, adding enough milk to moisten if very stiff. Whisk the egg white until stiff, and fold in.
3. Divide the mixture between greased bun tins and dust with caster sugar. Bake in a hot oven, 220°c, Gas 7, for about 20 minutes, until well risen and firm to the touch.

Bara Brith

Bara Brith (without yeast)

450g (1lb) mixed dried fruit
300ml (½ pint) cold tea
2 tablespoons marmalade
1 egg, beaten
6 tablespoons soft brown sugar
1 teaspoon mixed spice
450g (1lb) self-raising flour
honey to glaze

1. Soak the fruit overnight in the tea, or for at least 2 hours.
2. Mix in the marmalade, egg, sugar, spice and flour. Spoon into a greased 900g (1 lb) loaf tin and bake in a warm oven, 170°c, Gas 3, for 1½ hours, or until the centre is cooked through. Check from time to time that the top doesn't brown too much, and cover with a sheet of foil or move down a shelf in the oven, if necessary.
3. Once cooked, leave the Bara Brith to stand for 5 minutes then tip out of the tin on to a cooling tray. Using a pastry brush, glaze the top with honey.
4. Serve sliced, with salted butter and some tasty farmhouse Welsh cheddar.
5. Store in an airtight tin.

Welsh Cakes

Makes about 12

225g (8oz) self-raising flour
a pinch of salt
1 teaspoon mixed spice
100g (4oz) butter or 50g (2oz)
   each butter and lard
75g (3oz) caster sugar
   and extra for dredging
75g (3oz) mixed currants and sultanas
1 egg, beaten
1 teaspoon runny honey

1. Sieve the flour, salt and spice into a mixing bowl. Rub in the fats until the mixture looks like fine breadcrumbs

2. Add the sugar and dried fruit. Pour in the beaten egg and honey and stir to make a fairly firm dough.

3. On a floured board, roll or press the dough out to approximately 5mm (½") thick. Cut into discs with a 4 or 5cm (1½" or 2") cutter.

4. Bake the Welsh Cakes on a medium hot griddle, turning once, until golden brown on both sides but still a little soft in the middle.

5. Dredge with caster sugar.

Winter

They bring some fowl at Michaelmas,

A dish of fish at Lent,

At Christmas a capon,

At Michaelmas a Goose,

And something else at New Year's Eve,

For fear the lease fly loose.

During the cold winter months, we should nurture ourselves and eat comforting foods like thick cawl, homemade steak and leek pie, and steamed Snowdon pudding. Christmas brings a much needed celebration; alas for all the commercialism, but getting back to the seasonal and simple dishes can be very rewarding.

Traditional Welsh Cawl

1 breast of lamb
1 onion, cut in half
1 carrot
1 parsnip
1 bay leaf
A bunch of parsley, stems
   and tops used separately
1 large leek, white and
   green part separated
3 carrots, peeled and cubed
2 parsnips, peeled and cubed
2 turnips, peeled and cubed
A bunch of fresh winter savory or sage
salt and pepper

1. Roast the breast of lamb in a hot oven for an hour and a half, so that the skin is crisp and brown.
2. Leave to cool then strip the lamb off the bones, removing the fatty layers and saving the bones and meat.
3. Make up some stock from the bones, add the onion, carrot, parsnip, bay leaf and parsley stalks, and simmer for a good two hours then leave to cool, and skim the fat from the surface.
4. Gently fry the cubed carrots, parsnips, turnips and the bottom, white half of the leek, in a tablespoon of the lamb fat. Pour in the stock, add the lean lamb, cut into dice, and the chopped parsley and savory.
5. Simmer for a further 20 minutes.
6. Season well and serve the cawl with chunks of fresh bread.
7. Alternatively, leave overnight for the flavours to develop.

Lobsgows

450g (1lb) chuck steak,
　　cut into 1 inch cubes
marrow bone
3 medium onions, peeled and sliced
2 large carrots, peeled and cut into
　　large chunks
1 small swede, peeled and
　　cut into chunks
3 large potatoes, peeled and diced
2 medium leeks, washed and diced
1.2 litres (2 pints) hot water
salt and freshly milled black pepper

1. In a large pan, simmer
   the steak, marrow bone
   and onions gently in
   1.2 litres (2pints) of
   water for about 1½ hours.
2. Add seasoning and the
   prepared vegetables, and
   simmer for a further hour.
3. Correct the seasoning
   and serve, on a cold
   winter's day, with plenty
   of fresh, crusty bread.

Bacon-wrapped Leeks

4 medium leeks, washed and cut into 3 pieces
12 rashers of streaky bacon

1. Blanch the leeks in boiling
   salted water for 4–5 minutes
   until almost tender.
2. Refresh under cold running
   water and drain.
3. Wrap each portion of leek
   with a rasher of bacon, grill
   under a medium heat for 10
   minutes until the bacon is crispy.

Pembrokeshire Potato Cake with Bacon and Laver bread, topped with Poached Egg

175g (6oz) potatoes, peeled, boiled and mashed
100g (4oz) self raising flour
2 eggs
25g (1oz) melted butter
2 tablespoons laver bread seaweed (omit if hard to source)
6 rashers smoked back bacon, grilled and cut into small dice
salt and freshly ground black pepper

For the Poached Egg
4 free range or organic eggs

To garnish
½ tomato, deseeded and finely chopped
1 tablespoon chopped parsley

1. Combine the mashed potato, flour, eggs and butter to make a thick batter. Add the laver bread and ½ the bacon and season well.
2. Griddle the batter to make 4 small pancakes.
3. Poach the eggs and arrange one on top of each pancake.
4. Garnish with the chopped tomato, parsley and the rest of the bacon.

87

Welsh Cheese, Leek and Bacon Puffs

Welsh Cheese, Leek and Bacon Puffs

50g (2oz) butter
4 rashers of bacon, diced
1 leek, washed and chopped
50g (2oz) plain flour
300ml (½ pint) full fat milk
50g (2oz) Welsh cheddar, Llanboidy,
   Llangloffan, Hen Sir
2 teaspoons wholegrain mustard
100ml (4 fl oz) white wine

For the Pastry
150g (5oz) plain flour
100g (4oz) butter
pinch of salt
300ml (½ pint) water
4 eggs, beaten together
50g (2oz) Welsh Gouda –
   Teifi, Penbryn, grated
good pinch of chilli or cayenne pepper

Pastry

1. Put the butter and water into a pan and heat gently, until the butter melts, then raise the heat and rapidly bring the mixture to the boil.

2. Take the pan off the heat and pour all the flour in at once. Beat hard with a wooden spoon, until all the lumps have dispersed and the mixture comes away from the sides of the pan, but don't over beat, or the butter will run.

3. Leave the pastry to cool slightly before adding the eggs, a little at a time, beating well between each addition. The pastry should be shiny, and thick enough to hold its shape.

4. Add the Welsh Gouda cheese and cayenne pepper and leave to cool.

5. Spoon or pipe the pastry onto baking sheets (in knobs the size of a cherry) and bake for 20 minutes at 210°c, Gas 7, until crisp and golden.

6. Cool the buns before filling.

Filling

1. Melt the butter in a pan and cook the bacon till crisp.
2. Add the leek and cook till soft.
3. Stir in the flour to make a roux. Add the milk and stir till smooth.
4. Add the grated cheddar, mustard and white wine.
5. Leave the filling to cool.
6. To make up the puffs, fill a spoonful of the bacon, leek and cheese mixture into each bun and serve warm.

Welsh Rarebit
Caws pob

225g (8oz) strong-flavoured cheddar
25g (1oz) butter, melted
1 tablespoon Worcestershire sauce
1 tablespoon English mustard
1 tablespoon flour
4 tablespoons beer
4 slices wholemeal toast
cayenne pepper

1. Grate the cheese and mix with the remaining ingredients to a firm paste.
2. Spread over the 4 slices of toast and grill gently until the topping is cooked through and well-browned.
3. Garnish with cayenne pepper

Welsh Rarebit Caws pob

Smoked Fish and Chive Omelette

Fish and Shellfish
Smoked Fish and Chive Omelette

225g (8oz) smoked haddock, cod,
    trout or sewin (Welsh sea trout)
3 tablespoons crème fraiche
1 tablespoon chopped chives
5 eggs
2 tablespoons freshly grated Teifi
    (Welsh Gouda) cheese
salt and freshly ground black pepper
25g (1oz) butter

1. If the fish is not already cooked, steam or microwave the haddock until just opaque, then flake the flesh, removing the skin and bones. Mix the fish with the crème fraiche and chives, saving some crème fraiche and chives for garnish.

2. Separate the eggs. Beat the yolks together with some salt and pepper. In a separate clean bowl, whisk the egg whites until stiff, and fold into the yolks with the haddock and half the cheese.

3. Preheat the grill. Heat the butter in an omelette or frying pan. When it stops sizzling, pour in the egg mixture, and stir to encourage the omelette to cook evenly. When it begins to set, scatter over the remaining cheese. Finish cooking under the grill.

4. Garnish with a little crème fraiche and chives.

1 large onion, sliced
2 cloves garlic, crushed
300ml ($\frac{1}{2}$ pint) fish, chicken or
    vegetable stock
3 tablespoons balsamic vinegar
$\frac{1}{2}$ teaspoon crushed red chillies
$\frac{1}{2}$ tablespoon fresh rosemary,
    finely chopped
3 tablespoons fresh parsley,
    finely chopped
2 tins x 400g (14 oz) chopped
    tomatoes
450g (1lb) cod, skinned, boned
    and cut into 2.5 cm (1") cubes
a few well scrubbed mussels
salt and freshly ground pepper to taste

To serve

toasted slices fresh French bread
chopped parsley

Spicy Cod Casserole

1. Combine the onion, garlic, stock, vinegar and chillies in a large pan. Cover and bring to the boil.

2. Boil for 5–7 minutes. Uncover, lower the heat and simmer until the onions are tender and the liquid almost gone. Stir in the herbs and cook for a minute then add the tomatoes and simmer for 15 minutes.

3. Add the fish and mussels and season to taste.

4. Simmer for 5–7 minutes, until the fish is just cooked through and the mussels open.

5. To serve: place a slice of toast in a shallow soup dish, ladle the fish and sauce over the toast and sprinkle with parsley.

Spicy Cod Casserole

Crab and Cockle Fishcakes

Crab and Cockle Fishcakes

275g (10oz) crab meat and cockles
(in any proportion)
175g (6oz) fresh white breadcrumbs
1 teaspoon Cajun spices
1 tablespoon mayonnaise
2 sprigs fresh basil

for coating and frying
plain flour, beaten egg, fresh
breadcrumbs, vegetable oil

1. Thoroughly mix all the ingredients.
2. Divide into small patties and place on a tray. Chill for half an hour.
3. Roll each fishcake in flour, beaten egg and fresh breadcrumbs and then shallow fry in oil until golden brown on both sides.

Meat, Poultry and Offal
Spiced Breast of Welsh Lamb

1 breast of lamb
2 teaspoons salt
1 teaspoon black pepper
a pinch of ground allspice and cloves

Dry marinade
40g (1½ oz) rock sea salt
6g (½ oz) saltpetre (optional)
12g (½ oz) soft brown sugar

1. Remove the bones from the breast of lamb, cut away excess fat and sprinkle over the salt, black pepper, ground allspice and cloves.
2. Roll up the lamb and tie or secure with cocktail sticks. Rub over the dry marinade mixture of rock salt, saltpetre and soft brown sugar. Turn the lamb and leave in the fridge for up to a week, recoating with the marinade mixture daily.
3. Rinse the lamb well under a cold tap, place in a pan, cover with cold water and simmer for at least 1 hour, until soft when pierced. Leave the lamb to cool in the cooking liquid, then drain and transfer to the fridge, and cover with a weight for at least 12 hours.
4. Serve cold, thinly sliced with sweet, fruity chutney.

Sirloin of Welsh Black Beef with Leek Batter Puddings

1.4–1.8kg (3–4 lbs) sirloin of Welsh black beef, boned and rolled

Leek Batter Puddings
1 leek, washed and finely chopped
300ml (1/2 pint) milk
100g (4oz) plain flour
1 egg
salt and pepper

1. Place the meat into a hot oven, 230°c, Gas mark 8, and, after 15 minutes, reduce the heat to 200°c, Gas mark 6. When cooking, allow 15 minutes per pound, and an extra 15 minutes. (A 1.4kg (3lb) joint will therefore take one hour to cook).

2. Once cooked, allow the beef to rest, in the tin, in a warm place for a further 15 minutes, for the juices to settle. This also makes the meat firmer to carve.

3. About 20 minutes before you are ready to dish up, pop the batter puddings into the oven on a rack above the meat.

1. Cook the leek in a minimum of water in a saucepan, until barely soft. Leave to cool.

2. Make a batter with the milk, flour, egg and seasoning. Add the leek.

3. Pour the batter into a hot 12-bun-tin tray which has a little oil in the bottom of each compartment.

4. Bake for 20 minutes until risen and golden brown.

To serve: Dish up the meat onto a carving dish, pour the meat jus into a serving jug and arrange the leek batter puddings around the joint.

Salt Duck with Onion Sauce

1.75–2.25kg (4–5lb) duck
100g (4oz) sea salt
2 medium onions, peeled chopped
50ml (2fl oz) water
1 level tablespoon plain flour
300ml (½ pint) milk

1. Rub the salt well into the flesh of the duck, turning and recoating every day for 3 days. Keep the duck in a cool place throughout the salting process.
2. Thoroughly rinse the salt off the duck and place it into a large pan or casserole. Pour over cold water to cover, bring to the boil and simmer very gently for 1½ hours, turning over half way through.
3. Stew the chopped onion very, very gently in water for a bout 15 minutes, until tender (it may be necessary to press some greaseproof paper down on top of the onions to retain moisture). Strain off the liquid and blend it with the flour, using a whisk. Add the milk and then return the mixture to the onions. Bring the onion sauce to the boil. Simmer for a minute or two, in order to cook the flour and thicken the sauce. Either liquidise, or sieve, the sauce, and taste for seasoning.
4. Serve the duck sliced, with the sauce.
5. A fruity chutney tastes great with this dish.

Casserole of Heart with Fresh Rosemary

4 lamb or 2 calf hearts
juice of a lemon
225g (8oz) onions, peeled and sliced
2 medium cooking apples,
    peeled and cored
2–3 rounded tablespoons
    plain flour
50g (2oz) butter
salt and black pepper
2 bay leaves
150ml (¼ pint) cider
1 tablespoon fresh rosemary,
    chopped
1 level teaspoon caster sugar

1. Cut the hearts into slices, about ½ inch thick, and remove all fat, gristle and blood vessels.

2. Put the slices in a basin with the lemon juice and leave to marinate for 30 minutes. Dry the heart slices and coat them with flour, then fry them in the butter, in a flameproof casserole, over high heat. Add the onion and continue frying until pale golden. Season well with salt and freshly ground pepper. Add the bay leaves and the cider.

3. Cover the heart slices with the apple and sprinkle them with the rosemary and sugar.

4. Put the lid on the casserole and simmer over a low heat on top of the stove, or in a pre-heated oven at 150°c, Gas mark 2, for about 1 hour or until tender.

5. When cooked, remove the bay leaves and stir the apple slices into the sauce.

6. Serve the casseroled hearts with creamed potatoes.

Tripe and Onions

450g (1lb) tripe, cut into ½" pieces
3 large onions, peeled and chopped
600ml (1 pint) milk
25g (1oz) butter
25g (1oz) plain flour
salt and black pepper
A rounded tablespoon
  finely chopped parsley

1. Put the tripe and onions in a heavy-based pan; pour over the milk to cover (if necessary, top up with water). Cover the pan tightly with a lid and cook over a gentle heat for about 2 hours, or until the tripe is tender.
2. Strain through a coarse sieve and set aside about 1 pint of the liquid.
3. Make a roux from the butter and flour and gradually blend in the liquid. Bring to the boil and season to taste with salt and ground pepper.
4. Re-heat the tripe and onions in the sauce, add the parsley and serve.

675g (1½ lb) lean stewing steak
225g (8oz) pig's kidney
2 leeks, washed and chopped
2 tablespoons seasoned flour

For the suet crust pastry
225g (8oz) self raising flour
pinch of salt
110g (4oz) shredded suet
150ml (½ pint) cold water (approx)

Steak, Kidney and Leek Pudding

First make the pastry

1. In a bowl, mix the flour, salt and suet together then stir in the water until you have a light, elastic dough. Turn the dough on to a lightly floured surface, sprinkle with a little flour and knead lightly to shape into a ball. Cover and leave to rest for 10–15 minutes.

2. Cut the beef and kidney into ½" chunks. Toss in the seasoned flour and mix with the chopped leeks.

3. Using ½ of the suet pastry, roll it out to a circle ½" thick. Grease a 900 ml (1½ pint) pudding basin well and fit the pastry to the bottom and sides, allowing it to overhang the edge of the basin by about ½".

4. Spoon in the meat and leek mixture with plenty of extra seasoning.

5. Pour enough cold water to cover, to a depth of three quarters of the basin.

6. Roll out the remaining pastry to a circle and fit on top of the basin. Damp the edges of the suet crust lining and pinch together to seal.

7. Cover the top of the basin with double thickness of buttered greaseproof paper, folding in a wide pleat across the centre, to allow the pudding to rise; secure the paper tightly with string.

8. Put the pudding in a saucepan and pour boiling water around it until it reaches one third up the sides.

9. Steam briskly for 3–4 hours, topping up with boiling water.

10. Serve the pudding accompanied by green vegetables.

Vegetables, Salads and Vegetarian Dishes

Punchnep

450g (1lb) potatoes, peeled
450g (1lb) baby turnips, scrubbed, topped and tailed
50g (2oz) butter
salt and freshly ground pepper
50ml (2fl oz) cream, buttermilk or yoghurt (optional)

To garnish
chopped parsley

1. Cut the potatoes and turnips into chunks about 2.5 cm (1 in) diameter. Put in a large pan of cold, salted water, bring to the boil and simmer until tender.

2. Drain the cooked vegetables and, whilst still warm, mash together with the butter and plenty of seasoning.

3. Serve the punchnep as it is or, for a real treat, stir in some cream, buttermilk or yoghurt. Garnish with the parsley.

Apple Glazed Parsnip Puree

Apple Glazed Parsnip Puree

675g (1½ lb) parsnips, peeled or
   scrubbed and chopped into chunks
sea salt and freshly ground black
   pepper
1 large cooking apple
juice of ½ lemon
15 ml (1 tablespoon) soft brown sugar

1. Steam, boil or microwave the parsnips in a minimum of water. Drain, then mash to a purée and season well. Spread half the purée over the base of a shallow gratin dish.
2. Peel, core and very thinly slice the apple. Cover the purée with half the apple slices. Repeat these layers once more, arranging the remaining apple slices neatly on the top and sprinkling over the lemon juice and sugar.
3. Bake in a pre-heated moderate oven, 180°c, Gas mark 4, for about 30 minutes, or until the apple slices are soft and beginning to brown.

Onion Cake
Teisen Nionod

1 bay leaf
900g (2lb) potatoes, peeled, finely sliced and placed into cold water to prevent discoloration
225g (8oz) onions, peeled and finely sliced
75g (3oz) butter, melted
salt and freshly ground black pepper

1. Butter an 18cm (7in) deep cake tin and put the bay leaf in the bottom.
2. Place a layer of potatoes over the base. Add a layer of onions, brush with melted butter and season well with salt and pepper. Continue these layers, finishing with a layer of potatoes.
3. Press the cake down well into the tin, brush the top with butter and cover with foil. Bake in a hot oven, 220°c, Gas mark 7, for about one hour, or until the potatoes are soft. Remove the foil for the last 10 minutes, to brown the surface. Turn the cake out to serve.
4. Grated cheese could be added to the onion cake to give it a more substantial flavour.

Onion Cake (Teisen Nionod)

Braised Onions with Glamorgan Stuffing

4 large onions, peeled
150g (5oz) fresh breadcrumbs
1 small leek, washed and finely
   chopped
75g (3oz) Caerphilly cheese, grated
75g (3oz) Glamorgan ham,
   chopped
1 tablespoon of fresh parsley,
   chopped
salt and pepper
pinch of dry mustard
2 eggs
butter to glaze
150ml (5fl oz) stock

1. Boil the onions for 6–8 minutes and then drain.
2. When cool enough to handle, carefully hollow out some of the centres. Chop this and mix with fresh breadcrumbs, chopped parsley, seasoning, mustard, cheese, ham, leek and the egg to bind.
3. Press the stuffing into the hollowed out onions.
4. Place them in a lightly greased ovenproof dish. Brush with a little melted butter. Spoon some stock over to a depth of 10mm (½ inch). Cover with kitchen foil.
5. Bake at 190°c, Gas mark 5, for 45 minutes. Baste once or twice during cooking.
6. Serve hot.

Monmouth Meringue Pudding

Grated rind of 1 lemon
2 tablespoons caster sugar
25g (1oz) butter
450ml (15fl oz) milk
175g (6 oz) fresh white breadcrumbs
3 egg yolks
4–5 teaspoons raspberry jam, or
100g (4oz) fresh seasonal fruit –
    strawberries, cherries etc

For the topping
3 egg whites
3 tablespoons caster sugar

1. Add the lemon rind, sugar and butter to the milk and bring to the boil. Pour this mixture over the breadcrumbs and leave to stand for 15 minutes.
2. Stir the egg yolks into the cooled bread mixture and spoon into four ramekin dishes or one larger dish.
3. Spread a layer of jam or the prepared fresh fruit over the top and cover with the meringue.
4. For the meringue topping: whisk the egg whites till stiff (so stiff that if you turn the bowl upside down they won't fall out), fold in the sugar with a spatula or metal spoon, and swirl the meringue on top of the ramekins.
5. Either put the ramekins into a moderately hot oven (200°c, Gas mark 6) for 10 minutes to crisp the meringue (but do watch them carefully) or bake in a slow oven, 160–170°c, Gas mark 2–3, until the meringue is brown and crisp – about 15 minutes for individual ramekins and 30 minutes for a larger dish.

Monmouth Meringue Pudding

Steamed Snowdon Pudding

100g (4oz) vegetarian suet
100g (4oz) white breadcrumbs
1 tablespoon corn flour or ground rice
pinch of salt
finely grated rind of 1 lemon
2 tablespoons lemon or orange
   marmalade
3 tablespoons caster sugar
3 well beaten eggs
3 tablespoons seedless raisins
a little butter

Wine sauce
2 tablespoons granulated sugar
½ lemon rind in one piece
2 tablespoons water
1 teaspoon corn flour
1 tablespoon butter
150ml (½ pint) Madeira, sweet sherry,
   Marsala or home-made sweet wine

1. Grease a 2 pint pudding basin with the butter and then press as many raisins on to the sides as will stick.
2. Mix together the suet, breadcrumbs, corn flour and salt, then add the grated lemon rind, marmalade and sugar.
3. Add the beaten egg and any remaining raisins. Carefully spoon the mixture into the basin.
4. Cover and steam for 50–60 minutes in a saucepan of simmering water, or microwave on high for 5 minutes.
5. Turn out on to a warm plate and serve with the wine sauce.

Wine Sauce
1. Boil the sugar, lemon rind and water for 2 minutes then remove the rind.
2. Mix the corn flour into the butter, and stir into the syrup, then add the wine and let it simmer for a few minutes to thicken.
3. Serve in a small jug with the steaming hot pudding.

Bara Brith Ice Cream

300 ml (½ pint) double cream
25g (1oz) vanilla sugar
75g (3oz) Bara Brith loaf
75g (3oz) soft brown sugar

1. Blend the cream and vanilla sugar together and whisk until thick but not stiff.
2. Churn in an ice cream maker until almost set. (If using the freezer, break up the ice particles in the cream two or three times during freezing).
3. Crumble or process the Bara Brith into crumbs and mix with the sugar.
4. Spread on a lightly oiled baking tray and bake at 200°c, Gas mark 6 until the sugar caramelises.
5. Leave to cool then break up into crumbs again with a fork.
6. Fold the crumbs into the ice cream just before serving.

Baked Apples with Frothy Orange Sauce

4 large Bramley apples
100g (4oz) mixed dried fruit
50g (2oz) Demerara sugar
   (adjust to taste)
1 teaspoon of ground
   mixed spice
2 tablespoons of
   runny honey

Frothy Orange Sauce
2 egg yolks
50g (2 oz) castor sugar
3 tablespoons orange juice

1. Core the apples and score the skin around the middle.
2. Mix together the dried fruit, mixed spice and honey and fill each cavity.
3. Place apples in a baking dish and pour warm water to a level just below the middle score line. Sprinkle each apple with Demerara sugar and loosely cover with foil.
4. Bake in a moderate oven, 180°c, Gas mark 4, for 20 minutes and then remove the foil for a further 10 minutes, to glaze the apples.

Sauce
1. Whisk the egg yolks and sugar together until thick and creamy pale.
2. Hold the bowl over a pan of gently simmering water, whisk in the orange juice and continue whisking until the sauce bulks up into a froth.
3. Serve immediately with the hot baked apples.

Baking

Bara Brith
with Yeast

450g (1lb) mixed dried fruit
200ml (7fl oz) cold tea
350g (12 oz) stone-ground
   wholemeal flour
350g (12 oz) strong white flour
2 sachets easy-bake yeast
1½ teaspoons mixed spice
175g (6oz) soft brown sugar
100g (4oz) butter, melted
2 eggs, beaten
½ teaspoon salt
honey

1. Soak the fruit for 3 hours in the cold tea (longer will soften the fruit so much that it breaks up in the mixer).

2. Brush 3 x 450g (1lb) tins or equivalent with oil and line the bottom with greaseproof paper.

3. Put the flour into a large, warm bowl and stir in the yeast, spice and sugar. Melt the butter and pour it into the flour together with the eggs and salt. Add the fruit and cold tea and knead gently for about 5 minutes, or until the dough is smooth and elastic.

4. Using a spatula, spread the dough to fit into the baking tins and leave to prove in a warm place for at least 2 hours. (Rising may take a long time due to the richness of the dough.)

5. Pre-heat the oven to 200°c, Gas mark 6.

6. Bake the Bara Brith on the shelf below the centre of the oven for 15 minutes; turn the heat down to 160°c, Gas mark 3, and bake for a further 45–60 minutes, covering the top of the loaf tins with foil if it browns too much on top.

7. Brush the cooked Bara Brith with warm honey to glaze. Serve sliced and buttered.

Oatcakes

Oatcakes

100g (4oz) wholemeal flour
35g (1½ oz) medium oatmeal
1 tbsp soft brown sugar
½ tsp salt
1 tsp baking powder
½ tsp cayenne pepper
75g (3oz) salted Welsh butter
Milk to bind, if necessary

1. Mix all the dry ingredients together.
2. Melt the butter and stir in with enough milk to make a fairly stiff dough.
3. On a board dusted with wholemeal flour, roll the dough out fairly thinly, about 0.25cm (½") thick, and using a 6cm (2½") biscuit cutter stamp into circles.
4. Bake on a baking sheet in a warm oven, 170°c, Gas mark 3, for about 25 minutes, until pale golden.

Gingerbread

450g (1lb) flour
3 tsp ground ginger
3 tsp baking powder
1 tsp bicarbonate of soda
1 tsp salt
225g (8oz) Demerara sugar
175g (6oz) butter
175g (6oz) black treacle
175g (6oz) golden syrup
300ml (½ pint) milk
1 large egg, beaten

1. Grease a 23cm (9") square cake tin, about 5cm (2") deep, and line with buttered greaseproof paper.
2. Sift all the dry ingredients except the sugar into a bowl.
3. Warm the sugar, butter, treacle and syrup in a pan over low heat, until melted, and pour into the dry ingredients, beating thoroughly with a wooden spoon.
4. Pour into the prepared tin and bake in the centre of a moderated oven, 180°c, Gas mark 4, for 1½ hours, or until well-risen and just firm to the touch. Leave in the tin for 15 minutes, then turn out to cool on a wire rack.
5. When cold, wrap in foil, without removing the lining paper. Store for 4–7 days before cutting into chunks, to give the flavour time to mellow.

INDEX

For a full list of books currently in print, send now
for your free copy of our new, full colour
Catalogue – or simply surf into our website at
www.ylolfa.com

Talybont Ceredigion Cymru\Wales SY24 5HE
ffôn 0044 (0)1970 832 304
ffacs 832 782
e-bost ylolfa@ylolfa.com